To

From Dublin 2019

XXOO
Carla + Dad

good vibes
COOKBOOK

TASTY, SUPER-HEALTHY RECIPES

INSPIRED BY IRELAND AND SURF TRIPS
AROUND THE WORLD

BY JANE AND MYLES LAMBERTH

good vibes
COOKBOOK

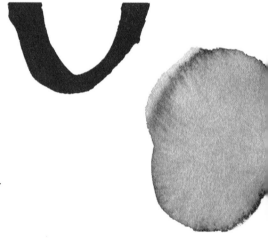

Jane and Myles Lamberth
With Shannon Denny

Published by Orca Publications

EDITOR: Louise Searle
COPY EDITOR: Shannon Denny
PHOTOGRAPHER: Mike Searle
DESIGNER: David Alcock
ILLUSTRATIONS: Paula Mills, David Alcock
PROOF READER: Hayley Spurway

PHOTOGRAPHIC CONTRIBUTORS: Sharpy, Matt Smith, Lorna Geraghty, Andrew Kilfeather

Good Vibes Cookbook ISBN 978-0-9930383-4-1

PRINTED AND BOUND: In China through Great Wall Printing
Published by Orca Publications
Berry Road Studios, Berry Road, Newquay, Cornwall, TR7 1AT, United Kingdom
TEL: (+44) 01637 878074 **FAX:** (+44) 01637 850226 **WEB:** www.orcasurf.co.uk

CONTENTS

A BIT ABOUT US.

Myles and I have always loved the outdoors. We met in Cornwall, when we'd both abandoned city life for beach life. After that we went on to travel the world – hiking in Nepal, snowboarding in Colorado, trekking in South Africa, mountain biking in the French Alps and surfing wherever we could.

When we embarked on our own business and opened up Shells Café in Strandhill on the west coast of Ireland, we made a conscious decision to remain true to what makes us happy. It turned out to be the best decision we made, as it guided us through the early days of setting up a business and all the stress and struggles that come with it. Often, after a super busy day with a long to-do list, we'd head straight out for a surf. Hitting the waves is always calming and refreshing, and clears the head to move on to the next job.

Now that we have our son Arlo in our lives, we feel it's even more important to pursue a healthy, active lifestyle. We have to lead the way for him and show him the best way to live. So now we sit down to family meals a good deal earlier, and try to encourage Arlo to try different veg and flavours. It's great when your child tastes something healthy and declares it 'delish'. We usually start the day with a smoothie and keep a good balance of fruit and veg in our diets throughout the week. However, like everyone we love our treats, so let's just say that moderation plays a strong role in our lives .

We feel that having Arlo to set an example for has helped us become more aware of what we eat, and we've found ourselves journeying down a path of healthy recipes, vitamin-packed smoothies and nutritious, tasty dinners with an explosion of flavours. The recipes in this book encapsulate the new lifestyle we are embracing – and we hope it encourages you to try a fit and healthy lifestyle, too.

The world is a book and those that do not TRAVEL read only a page.

SAINT AUGUSTINE

living the
DREAM

Since moving to Strandhill, Sligo, we have seen lots of young, creative people return home to Sligo or set up home here. Witnessing so much passion for a slower, more lifestyle-orientated existence has really inspired us. People are no longer accepting city life, which often involves high rents and long commutes. Instead we have seen a real investment in people's commitment to following their dreams, bringing them closer to the surf, the outdoors, nature and – ultimately – a healthier and more fulfilling life.

Some of our top inspirations in our area are:

Justin Carty - Shells Head Chef
We feel really blessed to have Justin running the show at Shells. A real gem of a person, he is so passionate about our business and treats it as his own. On top of running the kitchen, he also keeps sheep on the side of Benbulben mountain. Every year he gifts us with a sheep from his herd, fed on heather – the taste is amazing and it's such a treat to have him share the fruits of his labour with us.

Finn, of Finn's Fit Food book
Finn has paved a way as a freelance chef, cookbook author and general dream follower here in the West – proving not all opportunities have to be city based.

Dervla from Pudding Row
Not long after we opened Shells we stumbled upon Dervla's awesome organic café in the more remote coastal town of Easkey. Dervla is orginally from the area, and after a few years running her own café in Dublin, she upped sticks and returned to where her heart was and added a little slice of foodie heaven to our coastline.

Carolanne from Sweetbeats
We have always had great chats and inspiring conversations with Carolanne and were blown away when she had the courage to open a vegan-based café here in Sligo. With such a small population it was always going to be a gamble, but she has converted many of us meat eaters into choosing vegan a few days a week. With her delicious, warming dishes it is easy to avoid meat.

John and Elizabeth from Noji Architects
We were super-excited to see Noji Architects relocate from Dublin to Sligo; these serious creatives are contributing such beautiful designs within the Sligo landscape. It is great to find inspiration not just in food but in design and landscape too – and these guys are bringing it to Sligo in a big way.

Aoife from Bua Marketing
From time to time we bring in some marketing experts to help us out with Shells, and Aoife always brings her A-game. Orginally from Cork, Aoife relocated to Strandhill with her Sligo husband, and together they have renovated an amazing house that has been featured in magazines and online videos nationwide. Her business skills mean she is busy year round, choosing to take time when needed to enjoy the surf and strolls on the beach.

Salt & Soul Studio
We were delighted when this truly relaxing, dedicated yoga studio opened in Strandhill. What you could previously only find in London and Dublin is now available to us here in Strandhill – it's a totally Zen space with something for everyone. We often run Yoga

Brunch Clubs in conjunction with Salt & Soul, where we do a fun yoga class followed by a healthy community brunch in Shells. I love it as it brings people together and breaks down any barriers to trying something new. And it's so special to be able to partner with like-minded people in our village.

Strandhill People's Market

This market has been going for about two years now and keeps blowing us away with its array of local providers showcasing artisan gifts and food stalls. Its success highlights a real hunger to support local producers, and shows that people are keen to seek out homemade produce.

Voya Seaweed Baths

If Carlsberg did neighbours... Next door to us we have this amazing space where you can relax, have massages and listen to the ocean. Winters would not be as bearable without these guys. We can often be found dodging work for a quick surf with the Voya lads – and it's great to have such strong bonds with people who work around us.

All of these businesses are run by passionate young people, and they all offer something authentic here in Strandhill, Sligo. All genuine labours of love, you can feel the passion and drive behind each project, and that inspires us to be the best we can be.

Where we get our

Healthy food from...

At first glance, when I moved to Sligo I was a little disheartened at the apparent lack of good food shops to source healthy food from. However, now I realize that in a way we want all of our experiences to be convenient, shiny and easy, but that's not always the case.

We go to our local organic market every Saturday morning. Sometimes it feels like we have loads on and there isn't time to squeeze a visit in, but actually it takes so little time when you shop direct from the producers with no other distractions.

This shop usually sees us through till about Wednesday and then we might top up with Tesco organic range – it's not ideal, but you have to make the best of what you have.

Our local health food shop, Tir Na N'og is a great resource too, with a fab selection of dry goods and some veg. This is where we usually stock up on nuts, rice and cereals etc. In town, Kate's Kitchen is our go-to when sourcing more unusual ingredients and to grab a sneaky coffee on the go.

Of course we eat the homemade bread from Shells at home and sell that along with our own hummus, coleslaw and other goodies in the Little Shop located right next door to Shells Café.

I would encourage people to just make one small change to their weekly shopping experience and go from there. Small steps and little changes deliver big results.

I love that my market shopping has barely any plastic. I bring my own bags and the fruit and veg are all loose, so I have less waste as well as less packaging to recycle.

Another surprising thing for me has been the relationships you build by shopping this way. Having such interesting conversations with the ladies in Tir Na N'og, and Arlo getting a free apple from the sellers at the market – it all adds to our life experience and, again, forces us to slow down a bit.

Of course I am aware that not everyone can slow down and spend that time going to a few different places. During our peak times there is very little time for slow living, so during those spells I do online shopping with an organic supermarket that delivers nationwide.

I think you have to spend a bit of time sussing out what's available to you, what time and money you have, then make choices based on that. Are you passionate about less waste? Then market shopping is the way for you. Want to support local and small business? Then getting back to your local butcher or greengrocer will be really fulfilling... Small steps.

Myles

ginger

pistachio nuts

pumpkin seeds

quinoa

peanuts

mustard seeds

flax seeds

almonds

pecan nuts

goji berries

brazil Nuts

fruit

THE NEW CUPBOARD ESSENTIALS

You'll find a lot of new products in the supermarket these days. The health section has expanded from a couple of shelves to several aisles. So be adventurous. It's not hard to fit some new options into your cart and find a way to use them. Think outside of the box and integrate some of these ingredients into your everyday cooking. A lot of these products have similar properties to your old favourites, yet they bring more diversity, texture and nutrients to your diet and your taste buds.

The world is getting smaller and Western food is changing rapidly – in part because travel is so accessible. Embrace the exotic and explore new flavours. Here's our list of the new staples:

OI OI, OILS!

When it comes to cooking oils there are so many to choose from. Firstly you need to consider what you are using your oil for – is it baking, frying or dressing? Whatever the answer, always try to seek out pure, virgin, cold pressed oils. Generally, the higher the temperature you are going to bring the oil to, the less healthy it is for you.

Break away from traditional cooking oils and try:

Hemp oil
A super-healthy oil full of antioxidants, vitamin E and the good Omegas.

Rapeseed oil
Great for North West Europe if you're into food miles. Made in England and Ireland, this is a great 'local' oil with a high smoking point, making it great for frying. We use it in salad dressings, especially creamy-based ones or mayonnaise. We keep a great variety in Shells Little Shop, all of them pre-seasoned so that they are perfect to drizzle on local leaves, too.

Coconut oil
This isn't quite the miracle it's advertised to be, but it is definitely healthier than butter and it's super healthy in its raw form. When heated, it not only brings up the good cholesterol but the bad too. Better used in baking or raw cooking. It's most ideal use is as a vegan butter alternative in baked goods.

Avocado oil
This has low saturated fat, is packed with healthy fats and has a high smoking point, which makes it great for frying. It has a neutral flavour but is expensive.

Nut oil
Fantastic for salad dressings.

SWEETENERS

There's more to life than plain cane sugar.

When we look to more natural forms of sugars, our bodies can also get extra nutrients, rather than just a pure sugar rush. Sugar is all about the glycemic index (GI); refined sugars raise blood sugar levels the fastest, but there are some great alternatives with a lower GI.

Date nectar
Lower in calories than normal cane sugar, but still to be used sparingly. A bit like honey, date syrup has been known to have antibacterial properties.

Agave
This has a low GI so it takes longer to break down. It's more of a fruit-based sugar.

Vermont maple syrup
This is actually a source of antioxidants and can help improve digestion. Great in baking as it adds a nice flavour and blends well.

Coconut blossom sugar
This is all the rage in Australia and we can see why. It's made from the coconut plant and comes in granules too, so you can easily sweeten your tea and coffee with this lower GI alternative (refined sugar has a GI score of 60, whereas coconut sugar has a GI of 35). It also contains iron, zinc, calcium and potassium.

SEEDS AND BERRIES
Add during cooking or sprinkle on at the end.

They're also great in smoothies and porridge to kick-start your day.

Chia seeds
These guys are packed with Omega 3 fatty acids (the good fat). They help raise the good cholesterol, which helps protect against heart attacks and strokes.

Flax seeds
These are a high-fibre superfood with tons of antioxidants. Grown in Europe, they're friendly on the environment, too.

Hemp seeds
Great for Omegas 3 & 6, these guys also have easily digested proteins. Ideal for anyone on a plant-based diet and packed with B vitamins, these are a must-have on the shelf.

Goji berries
Originally from China, where they are used to treat liver and kidney issues. They have an unusual sweet

and sour taste, are great for the immune system and have a high-fibre content that aids gut health, too. Watch out though, as they are also an aphrodisiac!

Golden berries

Also known as the Cape Gooseberry. Similar to the goji, they are high in antioxidants and boost the immune system. Less common than goji, they can also be more expensive.

DAIRY ALTERNATIVES

Beneficial to the environment and to your health.

There's been a huge surge in the use of nut alternatives – and not just with plant-based eaters. Their main benefits are zero cholesterol and a low calorie content. In contrast to dairy-based milks, there is no use of antibiotics or hormones in the making of these products and – of course – they are lactose free.

Nut milks

Most cafés now offer a variety of nut milks for making milk-based coffees and porridge. An easy switch to improve the health of your heart, while still enjoying a latte.

Nut butters

Super-healthy alternative to butter. Great in baking and, again, low in cholesterol.

GOOD GRAINS

Step beyond plain white rice.

Start to choose wholegrains, which are packed with nutrients and also a great source of protein and fibre.

Oats

Great breakfast grain with a slow-release energy source. Low in cholesterol and full of nutrients, oats stabilise blood sugar levels so will keep you feeling full for longer.

Rye

A member of the wheat family, rye is often considered a superior grain if you're aiming to lose weight, as it binds with the water molecules and helps you feel full quickly.

Brown rice

Brown rice is gluten free, full of fibre and great for the heart. It also has a slightly nutty texture, which gives a new dimension to cooking with rice.

Barley

A member of the grass family, barley is a great source of fibre, which is easily available and helps aid digestion.

Quinoa

Grown in South America, this grain is gluten free and one of the few plant foods considered a complete protein, containing all nine essential amino acids.

FERMENTED FOODS

Nutrients that are good for your gut.

Basically these promote essential bacteria. Anything that is submerged in a brine during preparation kills off the dangerous bacteria, leaving the good bacteria to break down the sugars and starches, making digestion easier. It means that all the essential vitamins are retained, too.

Sauerkraut

Finely cut cabbage that has been fermented by various lactic acid bacteria. It has a long shelf life and a distinctive, sour flavor. It's like a plain kimchi. Awesome on a hot dog.

Kimchi

A traditional Korean dish made of seasoned vegetables and salt. Koreans eat it at nearly every meal. Mainly made from cabbage and spices. Try it with barbecued pork. Delish.

Kombucha

This fermented tea-based drink contains a large number of healthy bacteria known as probiotics. These line your digestive tract and support your immune system, as they absorb nutrients and fight infection and illness.

Keffir

Contains beneficial yeast as well as friendly probiotic bacteria found in yogurt. It has a tart and refreshing flavour and is similar to a drinking-style yogurt. If you find it hard to enjoy at first, stir it into your porridge and you will still get the benefits without having to drink it.

FLAVOURING

Wellbeing through great taste.

Miso paste

A traditional Japanese seasoning produced by fermenting soybeans. If you haven't been cooking with miso, then you've been seriously missing out. The salty paste can amp up just about any boring (savoury) dish, and it's also quite good for you. Miso taps into the 5th taste – umami.

Tamari sauce

A great alternative to soy sauce, as it has little or no wheat in it. It has a darker colour than soy sauce, is richer in flavour and is less salty, too. Great as a dipping sauce.

Raw cacao

Made by cold-pressing unroasted cocoa beans; a process that keeps the living enzymes in the cocoa and removes the fat (cacao butter).

Raw cacao looks like cocoa but it's not. Cocoa powder is raw cacao that's been roasted at high temperatures. This roasting changes the molecular structure of the cocoa bean, reducing the enzyme content and lowering its overall nutritional value.

Breakfast
of champions

power up
your day!

MORNING CLEANSE SMOOTHIE

This is a great morning smoothie. The lemon juice helps kickstart your digestion system, and it's super quick and easy to make. Feel free to adjust the quantities to your taste.

- ½ medium apple, cored and roughly chopped (peeled if not using a high-powered blender)
- 5 slices cucumber (skin removed if waxy)
- ½ lemon, juiced
- 1 heaped tbsp fresh ginger, roughly chopped
- 1 large handful baby kale, spinach, or other green of your choice
- 1 tbsp chia seeds (optional)
- A few sprigs of parsely (optional)
- Water
- Handful of ice

1. Pop everything into a blender, add enough water to get it moving and blend on high.
2. Add additional water to reach desired consistency.
3. Drink straight away.

BERRY, BEET & FRESH GINGER SMOOTHIE

One of my favourite smoothies before or after a run, even the most reluctant beetroot eaters will love this. Trust me! The coconut water is great to replace electrolytes, the beets and berries add beautiful colour, and the ginger gives it a little zing. Packed full of antioxidants and minerals, with great anti-inflammatory benefits, this is one for the whole family.

- 1 small roasted beetroot, peeled and quartered
- ½ cup frozen blueberries
- ½ banana (frozen if possible)
- 120ml (½ cup) unsweetened almond milk
- 120ml (½ cup) coconut water
- ½ inch of fresh ginger peeled
- 1 tbsp almond butter
- ½ tbsp flaxseed
- 1 tsp raw honey
- Handful of greens

1. Place all the ingredients in a blender and blend on high speed for several minutes.
2. Add ice and additional liquid if desired, and blend again.
3. Enjoy before a run for fuel, or after for recovery.

Quick, easy and packed full of green goodness

SUPER GREEN 'SUPERMAN' SMOOTHIE

Quick, easy and packed full of green goodness, this is my daily go-to smoothie. Dairy free, gluten free and vegan, this one's a winner every time.

- 400ml (1⅔ cups) coconut water
- 1 frozen banana
- ½ avocado
- Handful of spinach
- Handful of kale (remove stalks)
- 1 tbsp cashew butter
- 1 tsp agave syrup

1. Place all the ingredients in a blender and pulse until well combined.

2. Pour into a glass and serve.

3. Supercharge it with 1 tbsp chia or hemp seeds and 1 tsp spirulina.

perfection

BY THE SEA

We were super-excited to hear that Carolanne Rushe was opening a plant-based café here in Sligo. Jane says: "I love going to Sweet Beats and getting my fill of vegan foods that seem so simple, but are packed full of flavour and nutrition. It's my little health kick during the week."

We love Carolanne's smoothies as they are a meal in themselves, so we begged her to share one of her favourites:

RAW CACAO SMOOTHIE

SERVES 2

· 2 bananas, frozen
· 180ml (¾ cup) unsweetened almond milk
· 3 tbsp raw cacao powder
· 2 tbsp hemp seeds
· 1 tbsp maca powder
· 6 medjool dates
· ¼ cup ice
· Cacao nibs, hemp seeds and goji berries to garnish

1. Place all the ingredients in a blender and blend on high until smooth.
2. Pour into two cold glasses.
3. Top with cacao nibs, hemp seeds and goji berries.

THRIVING CAFÉ CULTURE

THE OUTDOOR LIFESTYLE IS A HUGE FACTOR THAT CONTRIBUTES TO HEALTHY AUSTRALIAN CUISINE. AN ABUNDANCE OF SUPER-FRESH, TROPICAL PRODUCE COMBINED WITH PAN-ASIAN INFLUENCES CREATES SOME AMAZING POST-SURF OPTIONS – FROM ZINGY SOUPS AND SMOOTHIES TO FRUIT BOWLS STUFFED WITH ACAI AND OTHER SUPER FOODS.

The sunny Australian climate encourages people to get up early for a run or a dip in the ocean. Home to one of the world's strongest and largest surfing populations, here riding waves is simply part of everyday life. Australians also tend to be competitive, so it seems that everyone is training for a triathlon, marathon or sporting event.

The café culture in Australia is thriving – a decent minimum wage means that everyone can afford to eat out, so huge support from the population is pushing café culture to the top of its game. And when it comes to cooking, Aussies are trendsetters, not followers, which means they are producing really different foodie experiences.

Myles' sister Paula – a graphic designer whose work appears throughout our books and in all the branding for Shells – lives with her family in Melbourne. Whenever we visit Paula our itinerary is typically filled with places to go for food and design, and we come home really inspired. And since she also lives near the Great Ocean Road, it's a perfect spot for surf trips!

HEALTHY BUDDHA BOWL

Finished with a lime coriander dressing, this healthy breakfast is jam-packed with protein and fibre without the fry up.

Don't be intimidated – there is a lot going on here but remember it's just a guideline to get you going and find your own style of healthy Buddha Bowl.

SERVES 4

- 2 ripe avos, peeled and sliced in two, with a splash of lemon (stops them going brown)
- 4 eggs, soft boiled for 4.5 minutes, peeled and sliced in two
- 8 kale leaves, chopped (we love using black kale)
- 200g (7oz) wild brown rice, or any healthy grain
- Olive oil
- 1 lemon, juiced
- Handful parsley/spinach, chopped

To garnish:

- Toasted almonds
- Flaxseeds
- Sesame seeds
- Chia seeds
- Alfa sprouts

For the dressing, blend together:

- 100ml (½ cup) good quality olive oil
- 2 cloves of garlic
- Large handful of coriander (you can use the stalks too)
- Salt & pepper
- 1 lime, juiced
- ½ a chilli, finely chopped
- 2 tbsp white wine vinegar

The best way to tackle this is to prepare all the ingredients first, then build the Buddha Bowl.

1. Pre-soak and cook the rice according to packet instructions.
2. Once cooked, allow to cool and stir in parsley, lemon juice, a dash of olive oil and a pinch of salt. Then set aside.
3. Blanch the chopped kale in a pot of boiling water for around two minutes, then drain.
4. While still warm, toss half the coriander dressing through the kale, plus a sprinkle of sea salt to taste.
5. Build up the bowl with kale and wild rice, balancing the avo, eggs, nuts, sprouts and seeds on top, packing it all in and giving a statement of healthy, clean living.
6. Finish with a drizzle of the dressing.

Eat and feel awesome for the rest of the day!

MANGO COCONUT RICE BOWL
WITH LIME, GINGER AND MINT

My favourite breakfast at the moment, love this!

A simple vegan recipe with amazing flavour, this healthy breakfast bowl goes down well as a dessert, too. I got the idea from a super-talented chef friend – thanks Katie Sanderson.

You need to start preparing it the day before, so plan ahead.

SERVES 4

- 160g (1 cup) short grain brown rice
- 2 tins coconut milk, left in the fridge overnight
- 1 tbsp honey, or your choice of sweetener (vegan alternative: agave)
- 2 ripe mangos, cut into strips (or any tropical fruit such as kiwi or pineapple)
- A thumb of fresh ginger, grated finely
- Zest of 1 lime
- Mint leaves, ripped
- A wedge of lime, to garnish
- Coconut flakes
- At Shells, we like to finish ours with coconut granola and more chopped fruit

1. Start the night before by soaking the rice in a pan of water – this yields a better texture once cooked.
2. Leave the tins of coconut milk in the fridge – the low temperature separates the coconut water from the thick coconut cream.
3. Drain the soaked rice, rinse away any excess starch and cook according to packet guidelines – usually around 20 minutes in boiling water.
4. Cool down after cooking, by running cold water over the rice or by spreading out onto a roasting tin.
5. Open up the coconut tins and scoop out the creamy stuff, saving the watery liquid for your next smoothie or curry.
6. Fold the thick coconut cream into the rice, and add honey, lime zest and ginger to form a porridge consistency.
7. If the rice is warm the coconut cream will melt, so make sure the rice is cold.
8. Taste and maybe add a pinch of salt or more honey/sweetener.
9. Serve in a deep noodle bowl, topped with sliced mango, seeds and nuts, ripped mint and a lime wedge.
10. Finish with a drizzle of honey and a scattering of coconut flakes

I like to eat mine fridge cold. The rice should keep for several days.

Enjoy!

No dairy.

Berry nice and healthy!

THE DAIRY-FREE BERRY SMOOTHIE BOWL

You might've heard of the acai breakfast bowl – a thick, smoothie-type breakfast made from the superfood acai berries – but let's face it, it's not easy to pick up acai berries in your local supermarket. So here is a berry-nice, easy breakfast bowl recipe, using readily available shop-bought frozen berries.

The concept is to make a thick smoothie as a base, then add lots of chopped fruit, seeds and nuts to keep you healthy, motivated and shake up your breakfast routine.

If you haven't invested in a powerful blender, this is the time to do so.

MAKES ONE LARGE PORTION OR TWO SMALL

- 340g (1 cup) frozen berries
- 1 frozen banana
- A few dashes of coconut water or nut milk (coconut, almond, soy etc)

To garnish:
- Coconut flakes
- Hemp seeds
- Chia seeds
- Flaxseeds
- Puffed quinoa
- Puffed brown rice
- Flaked almonds
- Healthy grains, seeds or pulses
- Extra chopped fruit such as kiwi, pineapple, strawberries or even dried fruits like dates or apricots. Anything goes, but keep it healthy.

1. Pop the banana and berries into a blender and blitz on low. It will look a little crumbly. The trick is not to blend too quickly. You can also use a hand blender.
2. Add coconut water or nut milk a few dashes at a time and whizz up.
3. Scrape down the sides with a spatula.
4. Once you've got a soft-serve ice cream texture, pop the mixture into a bowl.
5. Sprinkle the nuts, seeds, pulses and fruit on top.

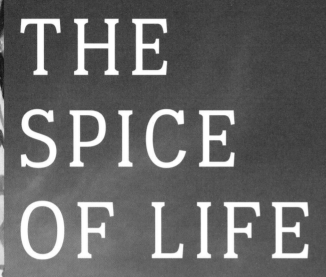

THE
SPICE
OF LIFE

SRI LANKA OFFERS THE EXPERIENCE OF THE INDIAN SUBCONTINENT, YET WITHOUT THE CHAOS AND WITH THE ADDITION OF SURF. There's a laidback pace of life here, which marries with the mellow waves. Sri Lanka is a great destination for intermediate surfers who aren't ready to charge Hawaii. There are plenty of reef breaks but the waves aren't too big and scary, and there are lots of new spots to explore that feel more welcoming than intimidating.

Food wise, the best surprise for us in Sri Lanka was the fish seasonings – amazing fish curries using ingredients we'd never thought of, like dried crushed prawns with coconut blossom sugar. Sri Lanka is home to a lot of spices and there's a huge heritage of medicinal plants. It's interesting to explore and worth going on a tour to find out all about the regional ingredients – from how ginger benefits your health and where mace comes from, to how Ceylon tea is made.

In Sri Lankan cuisine there's not much wheat – there's more gram and coconut flour. We really loved the local pancakes called 'hoppers', which are crispy, deep pancakes with either sweet or savoury fillings. You make them with rice flour and coconut milk in a wok, and they come out like a little wok-shaped basket. They're a great little breakfast dish.

Everywhere you go in Sri Lanka there are fresh coconuts for sale on the beach, so it's easy to rehydrate with a coconut water fix. Lassis (yoghurt-based smoothies) are another amazing discovery – they make it so easy to get a health kick when you need energy and fuel before a morning surf session. We loved having them for dessert, too!

TURMERIC LASSI

On our last surf trip to Sri Lanka we became addicted to drinking lassis. A major source of probiotics, a lassi should be on your weekly smoothie list.

So, what exactly is a lassi and is it just a fancy smoothie? Well, the difference between a lassi and a smoothie is simple: In a smoothie, fruit plays the leading role. In a lassi, yogurt plays the leading role.

This lassi recipe is loaded with turmeric, which is an immune-boosting powerhouse. Turmeric is also anti-inflammatory, an antioxidant, and a natural pain killer. If turmeric doesn't live in your spice cabinet yet, it should.

You can tone the amount of turmeric up or down, but if you follow the recipe below you'll get a sweet, creamy, lemon and ginger flavour with a little bite from the ginger.

- 245g (1 cup) plain kefir or plain organic yogurt
- 1 banana
- 2 tsp fresh ginger, grated
- ½ lemon, juiced
- 2 tsp fresh turmeric, finely grated
- 1 tsp honey
- 1 tsp vanilla extract or ground vanilla (optional)
- ¾ cup ice cubes (adds a nice frothiness)

1. Add all ingredients to a high powered blender and blend until smooth.
2. Top with a sprinkle of turmeric.
3. Serve in a thin glass, kick back and enjoy.

THE POWER OF OATS

WHY ARE OATS SO GOOD FOR YOU? THEY ARE A WELL BALANCED NUTRITIONAL COMPOSITION OF VITAMINS, MINERALS, PLANT COMPOUNDS AND ANTIOXIDANTS.

Oats contain a powerful, soluble fibre called beta-glucan, which reduces cholesterol. They are also good for your skin and are found in loads of skincare products. You can improve your blood sugar levels by eating oats, too.

TYPES OF OATS

ROLLED OATS:
These are just outgrowths, steamed and rolled into oats. They are a common breakfast cereal

STEEL-CUT OATS:
Oats cut into tiny pieces for quicker cooking.

STONEGROUND OATS:
You guessed it – ground with a big stone, resulting in creamier porridge.

WHOLE OATS (ALSO KNOWN AS JUMBO OATS):
Big, flat flakey oats that are better soaked first and take a long time to cook, but they are more wholesome so worth the extra effort.

VEGAN PORRIDGE

WITH VANILLA, CASHEW MILK & COCONUT BLOSSOM SUGAR

SERVES 2

- 140g (1 cup) porridge oats
- 475ml (2 cups) cashew nut milk (see page 61)
- 2 tbsp healthy seed mix
- ½ fresh vanilla pod
- 1 tbsp coconut blossom sugar
- 1 banana

1. Mix the porridge oats and nut milk in a saucepan.
2. Slowly bring to the boil, then simmer for a few minutes.
3. Finely split the vanilla pod in two, scrape out the seeds then add half of the seeds to the porridge.
4. Keep stirring with a wooden spoon, and add your mix of healthy seeds, such as chia, flax, pumpkin and poppy.
5. Reduce the porridge to your preferred consistency.
6. Serve in a fancy bowl and sprinkle a little coconut blossom sugar on top, with some sliced banana and a sprinkle of seeds.

Why not try a wintery alternative with hazelnut milk, poached winter fruits (such as pears and apples) and a sprinkle of Christmas spice? Yum.

YO SO EASY OAT BREAD

MAKES 1 LOAF

- 500g (2½ cups) plain yoghurt
- 750g (3¾ cups) porridge oats (use the yoghurt tub you just emptied)
- 2 tsp baking soda
- 2 tbsp oil – we use rapeseed
- 2 tbsp seeds, such as pumpkin or poppy seeds – save some for a pre-cooking sprinkle
- Knob of butter to grease tin

1. Preheat the oven to 200C/ 400F.
2. Mix all the ingredients gently, don't overmix.
3. Thoroughly grease a bread loaf tin.
4. Pour in the mix and bake for 40-45 minutes.
5. Don't forget to sprinkle some seeds on top before baking, for decoration.
6. Carefully remove from the tin.
7. Pop back in the oven to crispen up the edges.
8. Allow to cool.
9. Slice and butter up

This bread goes really nicely with cheese and chutney. This recipe is gluten free – but make sure your oats are gluten free to start with.

OVERNIGHT OATS
WITH OVER RIPE FRUITS

What can you do with that fruit that looks a little tired and wrinkly in the bowl? Hide it in a big healthy bowl of bircher muesli.

Bircher muesli is basically oats soaked overnight (or for a couple of hours) in juice, water and milk or nut milk. The muesli is then spiced and pimped up with fruit. All you need to do is grab your soaked oats, grate the wrinkly apple, smash up the black banana, squeeze out the juice of that shrivelled orange or squash the tired looking berries with a fork...

SERVES 2

- 60g (½ cup) oats – ideally jumbo oats
- 1 apple, roughly grated
- Pinch of cinnamon
- Pinch of nutmeg
- 2 tbsp nuts, plus more for serving
- 2 tbsp mixed seeds, plus a sprinkle to serve
- 150ml (⅔ cup) of liquid, like fruit juice, nut milk or water
- 40g (¼ cup) chopped, crushed, grated old fruit, like pear or raspberry
- 2 dollops yoghurt – optional
- Drizzle honey to serve - optional

1. Put oats, grated apple, cinnamon, nutmeg, seeds, nuts and liquid in a deep bowl.
2. Cover and chill for several hours or overnight.
3. Before serving, stir in selected over-ripe fruit, with a dollop of yoghurt.
4. Give everything a big stir, taste and season with more spice or liquid.
5. Spoon into a bowl and top with more fruit, seeds, nuts and a dollop of yoghurt (optional).
6. Drizzle honey on top.

ENJOY!

SO GOOD AVOCADOS

Versatile, creamy, healthy and delicious, avocados bring anything you're making up a level. So much more than a simple salad ingredient, you can blend them, bake with them or thicken things with them. A great substitute for dairy, you can use avocados in cakes or to make ice cream. Stacked with essential vitamins and minerals, avocados are one of the top fruits for your health, so instead of feeling like you're cutting things out, you're actually incorporating a whole, unprocessed ingredient that loads all the good things into whatever you're cooking.

ONE OF THE MOST POPULAR BREAKFASTS AT SHELLS IS GOOD OLD 'AVO ON TOAST'.

Avocado is rich in healthy, mono saturated fatty acids, vitamins K, C and E, as well as fibre and potassium. Some experts say that eating avocado can lower your cholesterol and triglyceride levels.

The first step to a good, smashed avo on toast is to use ripe avocados. When you squeeze them there should be a little give, or you can pop the stem off and check it has a dark green colour beneath it.

Choosing your bread

You want a good crunch to go with the softness of the avocado. Sometimes we rub a garlic bulb on the toast for extra flavour.

If you are having a tomato, chilli and avocado combo, you want a strong, yeasty bread, like a sourdough.

If you are having something more delicate like smoked salmon, cream cheese and avocado, then use a dark nutty bread, like soda or rye

For a greasy combo such as bacon, chorizo and avo, use bread that soaks well, like corn bread or batch bread.

DIFFERENT COMBO IDEAS

Bacon, chorizo, avocado, slow-roasted tomatoes and coriander on toast.
Tip – the slower you roast the tomatoes the better.

Smashed avo and smoked salmon on brown toast, with pickled cucumber ribbons.
Tip – use a veggie peeler to strip down the cucumber and pickle it in a mix of half white wine vinegar and half warm water, with some sugar to sweeten.

Spicy, zingy hummus, avo, sprouts and soft eggs on pita or flatbread.
Tip – make a shop-bought hummus extra zingy by adding a good squeeze of lemon juice and extra ground cumin.

Avocado and scrambled egg on toast with sticky, warm red pepper compote.
Tip – to make the red pepper compote, sauté two or three julienned red peppers in a pan for around 20 minutes, with two or three tablespoons of balsamic vinegar, brown sugar and a pinch of cayenne pepper.

WEEKEND CHILLI EGGS

One of our most popular dishes at Shells, this is the ultimate hangover cure. If you're having a big weekend with mates staying over, plan ahead and make up the amazing harissa paste and spicy tomato stew. Then it won't be a hassle to pull this dish together when you've got a fuzzy head on the Sunday morning.

- Sliced crusty bread and butter
- The freshest eggs, bacon and sausages
- Ripe tomatoes/ 2 tins tomatoes
- Celery leaves, or parsley
- Garlic
- Onions
- Vinegar (red wine or sherry)
- Cayenne pepper
- Harissa (a North African chilli and red pepper spread)
- Olive oil for frying
- Worcestershire sauce (optional)

For the harissa:

- 12 or more red-hot fresh chillis of various shapes, sizes and strength (if you are using dried chillies, soak in water for a few hours)
- ½ bulb garlic
- 2 tsp dried chilli flakes
- 1 tsp cumin seeds
- 1 tsp caraway seeds
- 1 tsp coriander seeds

(Toast all the seeds and chilli flakes in a dry pan, then crush in a blender to coarse powder form.)

- 1 tbsp red wine vinegar
- 2 or 3 tbsp olive oil or sunflower oil
- ½ preserved lemon, finely chopped (optional)
- ¼ tsp rose water (optional)

Harissa:

1. Heat the oven to maximum.
2. Roast the chillies and garlic for around 10-15 minutes until their skin starts to blister and blacken.
3. Take out of the oven and leave to cool.
4. Squeeze out the roasted garlic from their skins.
5. Add all the ingredients into a food processor and blend into a smooth paste. You will need to 'scrape down' the bowl a few times.
6. Be very brave and taste – it may need a pinch of salt
7. Jar it up and refrigerate – it should keep for a couple of weeks.

Simple tomato stew:

1. Dice the onions and garlic and lightly fry in olive oil in a heavy-based pan.
2. Add a couple of tins of tomatoes or a few fresh tomatoes and allow to cook for a couple of minutes.
3. Add cayenne pepper, sugar and a dash of vinegar and salt or Worcestershire sauce (think Bloody Mary).
4. Season with salt and pepper and gently simmer for 15-20 minutes.
5. Taste and season accordingly

Assemble the awesome chilli eggs:

1. Fry the bacon, egg and sausages.
2. Toast the bread, add a little butter and a thick layer of harissa.
3. Pile on the fried bacon, egg and sausages.
4. Smother in tomato stew and garnish with celery leaves (this helps cool down the dish).

Chill with Chilli Eggs in your belly!

Also try harissa on toast with melted cheese.

*pimp my

eggs

IRELAND'S WEST COAST IS
A SMORGASBORD OF WAVES
WAITING TO BE RIDDEN.

FANCY MUSHROOMS ON TOAST

Packed full of flavour and texture, this is a great vegetarian breakfast that any meat eater will love. Butter bean favetta is just a fancy name for flavoured butterbean mash. It's really worth including the mushroom ketchup as it cuts through the richness of the dish.

SERVES 4

- 2 tbsp butter
- 3 cloves garlic, diced
- 350g (3 cups) sliced mushrooms (chestnut, flat cap, shitake – any will do)
- A sprig of parsley, chopped
- Salt and pepper
- Good quality sourdough
- 4 eggs
- 1 tbsp white wine vinegar
- 2 tbsp mixed seeds (dry toasted in a hot pan for around 3 minutes)
- Mushroom ketchup (this can be shop bought or home made – check out the recipe on pg 58)

For the favetta:
- 2 cans (800g) of butter beans, drained
- 1 clove garlic, chopped/ grated
- 2 sprigs thyme, or parsley, leaves picked
- 3 tbsp olive oil
- 1 lemon, zested and juiced
- Large pinch of salt and a good twist of pepper

1. Heat a heavy frying pan on the hob and toss in the butter, followed by the diced garlic.
2. Cook for around 30 seconds, then add your mushrooms and shallow fry gently for around 5 minutes. Depending on your mushroom choice, you may need to add more butter along the way.
3. Finish with parsley or thyme (or both), a sprinkle of sea salt and a generous twist of black pepper. Then set aside the mushrooms while you make the favetta; they like to rest and it gets the juices to marry.
4. For the favetta, tip the butter beans, garlic, picked thyme leaves, olive oil and lemon juice into a blender and whizz until just combined – but retaining some texture.
5. Stir in the lemon zest and a good pinch of salt and pepper. Taste and season accordingly.
6. Bring a pan of water to simmer, ready for the eggs.
7. Pour a dash of vinegar into the simmering water and stir until a giant vortex opens up in the middle. Gently break the eggs into the centre and poach for about 3.5 minutes. Spoon the eggs out onto clean kitchen paper using a slotted spoon.

To serve:
Toast up your favourite artisan bread, spread the lemony favetta generously, pile on the mushrooms and carefully balance the egg on top. Finish with a blob of mushroom ketchup, toasted seeds and a few sprigs of green leaves.

Tuck in!

There won't be MUSH ROOM in your belly after this big breakfast…

RICOTTA HOTCAKES

Light and fluffy, with a slight tang from the ricotta cheese, these are a great alternative to standard pancakes.

MAKES ABOUT 15-20

For the batter:

- 250g (1 cup) ricotta cheese
- 125ml (½ cup) milk
- 2 large eggs, separated
- 100g (⅔ cup) plain flour
- 1 tsp baking powder
- Pinch of salt
- Vegetable/ nut oil for frying

Easy blueberry compote:

- 300g (1½ cups) blueberries
- 1 tbsp caster sugar

To garnish:

- 5 mint leaves, chopped
- Thick Greek yoghurt
- Honey to drizzle

1. First make the compote by squashing the blueberries with a fork, adding the sugar half way through. Allow to marinate for 5 minutes, while you cook the pancakes.
2. Grab a nice, deep bowl and mix together the ricotta, milk and egg yolks.
3. In another bowl, whisk the egg whites until stiff. (You can do this by hand to get your morning exercise!)
4. Back in the ricotta bowl, add the flour, baking powder and salt. Mix gently until combined.
5. Fold the beaten egg whites into the ricotta mix.
6. Try to keep as much air in the mixture as possible – don't over mix.
7. Heat a large frying pan, and with some paper towel smear a drop of oil all over the pan. Be careful not to burn yourself. Repeat this oil wipedown between batches of pancakes.
8. Drop in about 3 large spoons of batter at a time – they should spread out to the size of a beer coaster.
9. Cook for around 1.5 minutes, until the underside is golden and there are lots of bubbles on the top side.
10. Flip quickly with a spatula, cook for another minute and flip again for even, quick cooking.

Pancakes done!

To serve, pile up 3 pancakes and top with a big blob of yoghurt, a flick of fresh blueberry compote and chopped mint. Then drizzle the expensive, market-bought, hipster-made honey on top.

MOROCCAN SCRAMBLE WITH MERGUEZ SAUSAGES

Spice up your breakfast with some Middle Eastern flavours. You'll find merguez (spiced lamb sausages) at your local halal butcher. One of my favourites, they're a bit like lamb-flavoured chorizo.

We love Moroccan food and, of course, Moroccan surf. It's a fantastic country to explore, with warmer water, waves and stacks of colour and culture. It's easy on the wallet, too. Add it to your list of places to visit if you haven't already been there.

Now back to these eggs...

SERVES 2

- 6 eggs
- 6 tbsp organic plain yoghurt (hold back 2 to serve)
- 2 tsp olive oil
- 1 tsp ground cumin
- ½ tsp chilli powder
- 4 merguez sausages
- 2 thick slices of artisan bread, toasted
- Cherry tomatoes, to serve
- Spiced hazelnut dukkah, to serve (we make our own and sell it in Shells Little Shop, but it can be bought in good supermarkets)
- Cumin, grated garlic and salt (optional)

1. The secret here is slow-cooking the eggs in bain-marie style (a bit like melting chocolate).
2. To do this bring a pot of water to boil, then in a separate metal/ glass bowl beat the eggs, yogurt and a large pinch of salt together. Add the cumin and chilli powder. Then place the bowl on top of the pot of boiling water.
3. Stir slowly with a spatula or wooden spoon. The trick is to slowly scrape the egg mixture and fold it back in, rather than actually stir. You are trying to form large egg chunks.
4. Drizzle in olive oil as you go (roughly ½ a teaspoon at a time).
5. Meanwhile pan fry the sausages until they are browned, then place the cherry tomatoes into the pan with them.
6. Pop the pan into a hot oven to cook for a further 10 minutes.
7. Serve the sausage and scramble on hot buttered toast.
8. Top with the dukkah and the tomatoes.
9. If you want to go the extra step, mix some cumin, grated garlic and salt into the leftover yogurt and spoon onto the eggs. Salty yogurt sounds weird, but it cuts through the grease and is really popular in Middle Eastern culture.

MUSHROOM KETCHUP

Spread it on toast, shake on your steak or eat with your eggs – this ketchup is DA BOMB!

Taking your taste buds to another dimension, mushroom ketchup hits the fifth level of taste – or umami. Hailing from Japanese culture, this is basically when the savoury taste receptors bend to another level.

MAKES 700ML

- 500g (3 cups) button or chestnut mushrooms
- 6 cloves garlic
- 6 tbsp white wine vinegar
- 5 tbsp brown sugar
- 2 tbsp dijon mustard
- 2 tbsp Worcestershire sauce
- 10 anchovy fillets (optional but REALLY good)
- Black pepper

1. Combine the mushrooms, garlic and white wine vinegar in a food processor and blitz to a coarse purée.
2. Pop in a large pan and gently cook out the purée, adding in the sugar, mustard and Worcestershire sauce.
3. Stir for around 10 minutes on a gentle heat.
4. Finally, add in the chopped anchovies and cook for a further 5 minutes. If you decide not to use the anchovies you will need to add salt or soy sauce instead.
5. Add a good twist of black pepper.
6. Blend down further with a stick blender, until smooth and shiny.
7. Taste and season accordingly.
8. To preserve the ketchup, whilst it's hot, pour it into a clean, hot glass jar.
9. Seal with a lid and cool. It should last up to 3 to 4 weeks in the fridge.

APPLE AND MUSTARD KETCHUP

Warm and tangy, apple and mustard ketchup is
awesome with any pork or duck dish.

MAKES AROUND 750ML

• 2 large Granny Smith apples, peeled and diced

• 1 white onion, diced

• 250ml (1 cup) cider vinegar

• 250g (1 cup) caster sugar

• 3 cloves (not garlic, actual cloves)

• 3 tbsp Dijon or wholegrain mustard

1. Add all the ingredients except the mustard into a pot.
2. Bring to a gentle simmer, reducing the liquid vinegar content by half. This concentrates the flavour, giving it the tang. Around 15 minutes should do it.
3. Add in the mustard.
4. Spoon out the cloves.
5. Blend with a stick blender until smooth and shiny.
6. Taste and season with more sugar, salt or mustard, according to your taste.
7. To preserve the ketchup, while it's still hot, pour it into a clean, hot glass jar.
8. Seal with a lid and cool.
9. It should last 3-4 weeks in the fridge.
10. Enjoy with a bacon butty, pork burger or duck salad.

PEACH & CHARDONNAY LADY KETCHUP

MAKES 750ML

• 6/7 peaches, de-stoned and sliced

• 250g (1 cup) white sugar

• 150ml (¾ cup) white wine vinegar

• 100ml (½ cup) Chardonnay or Prosecco

• ½ vanilla pod

1. Place all the ingredients into a saucepan and bring to the boil.
2. Cook for 10-15 minutes, until the peaches are lovely and soft.
3. Drain the peaches and keep the liquid.
4. Remove the vanilla pod, put the fruit into a blender and blitz into a thick purée.
5. Slowly add the hot liquid back in until you get the correct consistency – it should be a smooth purée that holds its shape on the plate.
6. Sometimes the skin of the peach doesn't blend well, so if you are particular you can pass it through a sieve.
7. This delicate ketchup goes well with salads or in cold meat sandwiches.

PINEAPPLE CHILLI KETCHUP

Spicy and sweet with a real wow-factor, this is the
go-to condiment for any summer BBQ.

MAKES 700ML

• 2 small tins/ 1 large tin pineapple chunks, drained (but hold some liquid back)

• 8 red chillis, chopped

• Thumb of ginger

• 250g (1 cup) light brown sugar

• 250ml (1 cup) cider vinegar

1. Bang everything into a heavy-based pot.
2. Bring to a rapid boil.
3. Reduce the liquid until ¾ is gone.
4. Blend with a stick blender (I like to keep mine a little bit chunky).
5. To preserve the ketchup, pour whilst hot into a clean hot glass jar.
6. Seal with a lid and cool.
7. It should last 3 to 4 weeks in the fridge.

NUTS ABOUT nutmilks

Delicious and a great source of protein, nut milks have always been around, but a lot of the ones you can buy are sweetened. So while you might think you're getting a healthy product, the added sugars, sweeteners or preservatives can potentially outweigh some of the benefits.

The good news is that they're easy to make – all you need is a bit of pre-soaking and a good blender. You can make nut milk out of most nuts, but the most common choices are hazelnuts or almonds. It can be expensive to produce, but since nuts feature so much in Asian cooking, you can find the cheapest bulk buys at Asian grocery stores.

About half a kilogram of nuts will yield about a litre of nut milk. You can stretch the balance depending on how rich you like your milk. For instance, if you're using it to bake with, you might like it more watery. While if you're using it in tea or coffee, you might like a nice creamy texture. Coconut milk is possibly the most versatile option of all. When you stick it in the fridge it separates, so you can use the watery part in curries and the solid part in place of cream or butter.

Once you've tasted good, homemade nut milk, you won't go back. Not only do you know exactly what's in it, the quality difference is unbelievable.

NUT MILK

Nutting beats homemade nut milk and it's nut that difficult to make. A great alternative to dairy milk. Hazelnuts or almonds makes the best nut milks but you can use pecans, walnuts, cashew or even peanuts.

This recipe has a ratio of 1:4. For every equal cup of soaked nuts, use 4 cups of water when blending.

- 1 cup raw unsalted nuts, like hazelnuts
- 2 or 3 cups of water for soaking
- 4 cups of water for blending

1. Pop the nuts into a bowl and cover with water, ensuring they are completely covered.
2. Soak the nuts overnight, generally the longer they soak the better.
3. Drain the nuts and discard the water.
4. Blend the soaked nuts with 4 cups of fresh water until smooth.
5. Strain the nut water through a clean cloth, muslin or tea towel into a bowl.
6. Twist the top to give it a really tight squeeze.
7. The white liquid collecting in the bowl is Nut Milk.

Nut so bad eh?

Sweeten if you want with agave syrup or honey – depending on the nuts you use. Or add another cup of water to dilute and make the nut milk go further.

Refrigerate and use within 5 days.

matcha green

coconut flat coffee

alternative lattes

golden latte

COCONUT BUTTER COFFEE

Also known as 'Bullet Coffee', this combination of caffeine, protein and oil certainly provides a sustained source of energy.

- 2 tsp coconut oil
- 7g (1 knob) unsalted butter
- 1 cup of Americano coffee (espresso and hot water)
- 1 tsp coconut flakes (toasted) to serve

1. Blend together and pour into a cup.
2. Garnish with toasted coconut flakes.

MATCHA GREEN TEA

This is a firm favourite in Shells and great when avoiding caffeine. It will leave you feeling awake and energised without the shaky rush of caffeine. The matcha powder is said to be 100% more detoxifying than green tea because you ingest the whole leaf, not just the brewed tea. We sell it in little bags in our shop and it can be added to smoothies too. It's a little bitter, so when first getting used to it we usually recommend a bit of vanilla syrup or honey to take the edge off.

- 2 tsp matcha green tea powder
- 2 tbsp hot water
- 1 cup of milk (use any milk choice, we find coconut works great with it)
- 1 tsp vanilla syrup/ honey (optional)

1. Place green tea powder and hot water in a glass.
2. Whisk until blended (using a specific coffee wand whisk) or go for it with a fork.
3. Add some warmed milk (either microwave or warm on the hob).
4. Stir in vanilla / honey if required.

GOLDEN LATTE

At Shells, we love our golden lattes. We pop them on the specials board during the winter months when people need an extra kick. The smell of the spice is just so warming and turmeric also boosts the immune system, so why not give this a go? It's a great alternative to coffee when you are looking to keep your caffeine intake at bay.

Golden milk is basically a combination of turmeric and coconut milk.

- 240ml (1 cup) coconut milk
- 1 tbsp turmeric root, finely grated
- Honey, to taste
- 1 tbsp ginger, finely grated (optional)

1. Gently warm the coconut milk in a small saucepan. Do not boil. Add the turmeric and gently heat together.
2. Use a wire whisk or immersion blender to create a foam. Continue to stir until frothy and heated through.
3. Stir in honey and ginger, or sweetener of choice to taste.

Alternative method: To create an extra frothy latte, pour the contents into a high-speed blender instead of using a wire whisk or immersion blender.

NATURAL BUZZ

WE LOVE STARTING THE DAY WITH SOME EXERCISE AND HEALTHY EATING. IT GIVES YOU SUCH A MENTAL AND PHYSICAL BOOST FOR THE REST OF THE DAY. GETTING OUT OF BED TO FACE ANY EXERCISE CAN BE TOUGH, SO YOU REALLY WANT TO MAKE MINIMAL EFFORT TO GET ON YOUR WAY. WITH THIS IN MIND WE PREP THESE RAW BALLS THE DAY BEFORE, POP THEM IN A CONTAINER IN THE FRIDGE SO THEY ARE READY FOR YOUR HIKE OR SURF TRIP THE NEXT MORNING. IN STRANDHILL WE HAVE A WEEKLY 6AM GROUP HIKE UP THE MOUNTAIN, AND EACH WEEK SOMEONE WILL MAKE THE COFFEE AND PACK THE SNACK — IT'S A GREAT WAY TO CATCH UP WITH FRIENDS AND GET THAT OUTDOOR FIX.

GOOD PURE
ENERGY
RAW BALLS

Great for energy and totally raw-some, these will keep you going all day. Much better than a Snickers bar.

- 12 dates, pitted – Mejoule dates are the best
- 1 tbsp cacao powder (cocoa powder is ok to use, but don't use hot chocolate powder)
- 2 tbsp peanut butter (or any nut butter)
- 1 or 2 tbsp honey/ agave syrup (depending on how big the dates are)
- 120g (¾ cup) whole almonds
- Mixed seeds
- Desiccated coconut to roll (optional)

1. Place the dates, cacao powder and peanut butter into a food processor and blend into a sticky pulp.
2. Add the syrup slowly, whilst blending.
3. Add the almonds and blitz to reach desired chunkiness.
4. You are looking for a very sticky consistency – you may have to add more honey if it's too dry or more nuts if it's too wet.
5. Roll the mixture into brussel sprout-sized balls.
6. Pop the balls into a bowl of mixed seeds and desiccated coconut, and roll them around.
7. Set aside in a cool place.
8. Ready to eat straight away – or refrigerate ready for your outdoor excursion. These bad boys will last for ages, if you can resist them!
9. This is an easy recipe to double or triple if you need to.

BROWNIES HAVE MET THEIR MATCH WITH MATCHA GREEN TEA BLONDIES

A blondie is a brownie made with white chocolate.
But what we are actually making here is a greenie!

- 300g (10.5oz) butter
- 300g (10.5oz) white chocolate
- 5 eggs
- 350g (1½ cups) caster sugar
- 1 tbsp matcha green tea powder, mixed with 2 tbsp of hot water
- 150g (1¼ cups) plain flour
- 50g (2tbsp) golden syrup/ honey/ agave
- Handful pine nuts and pumpkin seeds to sprinkle

1. Melt the chocolate and butter together in a bowl over simmering water.
2. Remove from the heat.
3. Beat in the eggs, sugar, syrup and green tea sludge. Stir well.
4. Gently fold in the sifted flour. You should now have a bright green batter.
5. Pour the green batter into a lined (with baking parchment) baking tin – ideally a low, shallow dish.
6. Scatter pine nuts and pumpkin seeds on top
7. Bake for 25 minutes at 170 C/340 F until it's slightly golden on top and doesn't wobble.
8. You want to slightly under-bake the blondie to get that squishy fudge texture.
9. Remove from the oven and allow to cool completely on a wire rack before slicing.
10. These will keep for just under a week in the fridge – but trust me they won't last that long!

POWER
TO THE
FLAPJACKS

A great mid-morning energy boost, especially if you've missed breakfast. These are so good and keep for ages! They fly out the door of Shells Little Shop.

Tahini is basically peanut butter but made from sesame seeds.

MAKES 12 BARS OR 1 TRAY BAKE

- 500g (5½ cups) oats
- 200g (1 cup) dark sugar
- 340g (1½ cups) butter
- 3 large tbsp honey/ golden syrup (if vegan)
- 1 large tbsp tahini paste
- 1 large tbsp peanut butter
- 3 tbsp chopped peanuts
- 1 tbsp seed mix
- 1 tbsp dried small berries such as goji berries, cranberries or raisins

1. Mix the dry ingredients in a large bowl.
2. Line oven tray with oil and parchment paper.
3. Preheat oven to 170 C/ 360 F.
4. Melt the butter, sugar and syrup together.
5. Stir in the tahini paste and peanut butter.
6. Bring to the boil then turn down the heat.
7. Working quickly, stir in the dry ingredients.
8. Keep stirring hard, making sure everything is coated in sticky goo.
9. Pour into the lined tin and pat down with the back of a spoon
10. To get a great result, line the top with parchment paper and, using your hands, smooth the batter down to get a nice flat, even mix.
11. Bake for around 25 minutes until very golden and molten on top.
12. Remove and allow to cool completely before removing from tin.
13. Slice into long fingers and wrap with cling film – now you are set for the week.

Lunch

GREEN VEGGIE POWER SOUP

This spinach, broccoli and ginger soup is green to keep you clean.

SERVES 4-6

- 1 tbsp nut oil
- 2 tbsp coconut oil
- 3 cloves garlic, chopped
- 1 onion, diced
- 1 thumb of ginger, peeled and diced
- 1 turmeric root, diced (optional)
- 1 tbsp curry powder
- 5 celery stalks, chopped
- 2 large heads broccoli, chopped
- 2 potatoes, peeled and diced
- 1 large bunch kale, chopped
- 1 large bunch coriander
- 1 large bag of baby spinach (the more the better)
- 1 good quality veggie stock cube
- ¼ whole nutmeg, grated
- 1 tin of coconut milk
- 1 tbsp fish sauce
- 1 tbsp soy sauce

1. Grab a nice big heavy pot and fire it up on the hob. Add the nut oil and heat a little, then dollop in your coconut oil and melt it down.
2. Gently fry your garlic for 15 seconds to flavour the oil.
3. Add the onions, ginger and turmeric, and let them cook for a minute or two.
4. Stir in your curry powder, turn down the heat and allow the dry spices to cook out.
5. Toss in all the chopped vegetables plus the coriander and spinach, gently cook in the spiced oil for a few minutes and give everything a stir.
6. Fill the pot with water until the veg are covered by an inch or two.
7. Add your stock cube and let things simmer for 20 minutes or more with the lid off.
8. Test the potato pieces to see if they are nice and soft.
9. Blend well with a soup stick blender and scratch in the nutmeg, adding the fish sauce, coconut milk and soy sauce (to season).
10. Keep blending until smooth.
11. Serve with a garnish of coriander and chilli.

SPICY CABBAGE AND MISO SOUP

Mi-so happy with this healthy soup inspired by our Korean friends. We ate this in Hong Kong, while travelling through from one surf destination to the next. Miso is a great source of iron, calcium and plant-based proteins.

By using tofu we are going vegan with this soup, but if you're not that way inclined, you can make it with crispy pork belly.

- 750ml (3 cups) good vegetable or chicken stock
- Big thumb of ginger, peeled and finely diced
- 1 red onion, thinly sliced
- 2 tbsp dried chilli seeds (plus extra for garnish)
- 4 cloves garlic, sliced
- ½ savoy cabbage, cored and sliced thinly into strips
- 1 carrot, julienned into thin strips
- 2 scallions, finely chopped
- 2 tbsp miso paste (found in the deli store)
- 100g (4oz) soft silken tofu (optional)/ or cooked pork belly if you are feeling cheeky
- Soy sauce

1. In a deep pot bring the stock to the boil, then add the ginger, onion, garlic and chilli.
2. Simmer and let it all infuse.
3. Add the cabbage, carrots and scallions and simmer for a further five minutes until the cabbage has wilted.
4. Stir in the miso paste, taste, and add small amounts of soy sauce to your required taste.
5. Just before serving add in cubes of tofu or cold-cut pork.
6. Serve in shallow soup bowls with the cabbage piled high, and garnish with more dried chilli.

LEFTOVER ROAST CHICKEN RAMEN SOUP

Ramen is a traditional Japanese soup, often made with different types of noodles and broths, and traditionally served with an egg.

You over-indulged on the Sunday roast chicken and now it's Monday you want to be healthy again. What better way than to have a nice healthy soup using your leftovers?

SERVES 2-3

- 750ml (3 cups) chicken stock – homemade stock is best, see below for how to make it.
- Bunch of coriander, stalks separated from the leaves
- 1 chilli, chopped (save some for garnish)
- 100g (3.5oz) sliced mushrooms like oyster/ shiitake/ flat cap
- 3 cloves garlic, grated
- 2 tbsp light soy sauce
- 100g (3.5oz) ramen noodles
- Five scallions, sliced
- 2 bulbs baby pak choi
- Pulled leftover chicken (200g should do it)
- 1 thumb ginger, grated
- One soft boiled egg (optional but traditional)

1. Place a large saucepan over medium heat and pour in the stock.
2. Add the finely chopped coriander stalks, sliced chilli, mushrooms, garlic and soy sauce, and simmer for ten minutes.
3. Add the noodles, half the scallions and the pak choi.
4. Serve up in deep noodle bowls and garnish with shredded chicken, sliced egg, scallions, coriander leaves and fresh chilli.
5. Season with more soy sauce if desired.
Smile and feel satisfied after slurping up your noodles.

It's best to make this soup using chicken stock made from scratch. Here's how:

1. Start the night before when you are cleaning up after your Sunday roast.
2. Pick the rest of the chicken off the bone and pop it in the fridge for the soup the next day.
3. Break down the chicken carcass a little and pop it into a pot with a tablespoon of oil.
4. Gently fry up with onions, garlic and left over vegetable trimmings such as celery stalks, carrot peel, parsnip heads and any other wrinkly bits from the bottom of your vegetable drawer.
5. Cover with water and gently boil for a long time (min 1 hour).
6. Add a couple of tablespoons of soy sauce for seasoning and perhaps a pinch of salt – you are looking for a clean, light broth so it shouldn't be over seasoned.
7. Strain your broth through a colander, cool and refrigerate.
8. You can even freeze out portions in a zip-lock bag for future use.

OH LA LA VICHYSSOISE
WITH WEST COAST OYSTERS

This classic French leek and potato soup is traditionally served cold, but is just as nice served warm. Leeks and potatoes are loved by the Irish; I threw in the oysters to make the dish more unique to the west coast. This is a great recipe to impress your friends at a summer lunch party. The oysters are optional but highly recommended.

SERVES 4

- 50g (¼ cup) butter, split into two portions
- 1 white onion, diced
- 1 large sprig of thyme
- 1 bay leaf
- 4 medium leeks, white bits only – and don't forget to wash them well
- 5 large potatoes, peeled and evenly diced
- 1 litre of good quality chicken stock
- Salt and white pepper
- 1 tbsp dijon mustard
- 4 tbsp cream
- Four oysters, shucked and juices reserved

For the scallion dressing:
- ½ cup (100ml) sunflower oil
- Five scallions, thinly sliced
- Pinch of salt

1. Melt half the butter in a large pan over a low heat, add the onions, thyme and bay leaf, cook for a minute or two, then add the leeks.
2. Let the flavours marry a little, give the leeks some colour and stir every now and again.
3. Next add the potatoes and let them kiss the butter.
4. Add the chicken stock and bring to a gentle boil, reduce the heat and let it simmer for around 30 minutes.
5. Remove the twig of thyme and bay leaf.
6. Purée the soup with a hand-held blender or liquidiser, adding the rest of the butter and cream while you blend.
7. Have a little taste and season with dijon mustard, salt and white pepper.
8. Blend again and taste again – like a Michelin chef on a TV show.
9. If you're a real pro, you can pass it through a fine sieve for an extra smooth and creamy soup.
10. Refrigerate.
11. For the scallion dressing, heat up your oil in small pot until it's almost smoking temperature.
12. Carefully (and at a distance) throw in your sliced scallions. A huge sizzle and boil will occur, so watch out.
13. Switch off the heat, add a pinch of salt and let it cool right down. This dressing will keep refridgerated for over a week.
14. To serve, pour into your Gran's shallow bone china bowls, gently float an oyster on top and drizzle scallion dressing all around. Perhaps add wildflower petals, too.

This goes down well with a fine white Alberiño or Muscadet wine.

PACK UP A
picnic

When we're planning a picnic, we like to pack for the wow factor. From prepping to packing, here's a checklist to raise your al fresco eating game.

A BIG, BEAUTIFUL BLANKET

Splash out and get a huge, bright blanket that sets the tone. We have a particular blanket we use, which is a Zulu one with patches and quilting from South Africa. Throw pillows are a good idea, too.

FANTASTIC PLASTIC

There's basic plastic, and then there's melamine. The latter is more expensive but it's worth it because it lasts longer, washes well in a dishwasher and comes in great designs.

COOL CUPS

Cool cups. You can get your hands on some really decent plastic wine glasses these days. Spend a bit of money to find better quality stuff that you'll look forward to using. Myles' sister still uses their Gran's melamine-ware from the 1960s! They're beautiful cups and they're still going strong.

CHOPPING BOARDS WITH CHARACTER

Those little flimsy plastic chopping boards don't cut the mustard! We go to the local sawmill and get cheap slabs of timber, then spend 45 minutes with a sander going over the corners and the top. To seal the wood, all you need is rapeseed oil. These are great for display too – throw the food on in a pile and let people dig in!

THE PICNIC PRACTICALITIES

Have a little bag ready to go with all your essentials: rubbish bags, insect repellent, plasters, a torch, candles, a lantern, baby powder (to make it easy to wipe the sand off your body), sunscreen, multiple knives and a hat.

Finally, a top tip is don't be lazy. Decant food into bowls and go the extra step to make the moment memorable. Have a sense of style and go creatively wild!

Fruit waters...

Perfect for a picnic or a hot summer's day.

ROOIBOS ORANGE & HONEY ICED TEA

- Rooibos tea leaves (enough to make tea for two)
- 500ml (2 cups) water
- 1 orange
- 1 stick cinnamon
- 2 star anise
- 1 lemon
- 1 tbsp honey
- Ice

- Pop all the ingredients into a pot and bring to just before boiling point.
- Stir and allow to cool for 10-15 minutes
- Strain the liquid through a clean tea towel or sieve into tall glasses of ice.
- Garnish with the leftover orange, cinnamon and star anise.
- If you can get your hands on some apricot juice, add a little to the iced drink – this is fantastic!
- To spike, add apricot brandy.

MATCHA AND MINT ICED TEA

SERVES 2

- 1 tbsp boiling water
- 2 cups bottled water
- 2 tsp matcha green tea powder
- 2 cups crushed ice
- 1 lime, sliced
- Handfuls of mint
- 1 tsp agave syrup

1. Make a matcha paste by mixing the powder and the boiling water until full combined.
2. Using a cocktail shaker (or a large jar with a non-leaky lid), shake together the bottled water and matcha paste until there are no lumps.
3. Throw in the agave syrup and shake some more.
4. Add the ice, a squeeze of lime, handfuls of mint and shake, shake, shake your body.
5. Pour into glasses with extra lime slices and mint.
6. To spike it add some white rum.

FENNEL, APPLE & ELDERFLOWER ICED TEA

SERVES 2

- Fennel Tea
- Fennel fronds (leaves) or dill
- Apple juice (use equal parts fennel tea and apple juice)
- Splash of elderflower cordial

1. Make one very strong cup of fennel tea and allow to cool.
2. Once cool, add the apple juice, sweeten with elderflower cordial and serve over ice.
3. Ball up the fennel fronds and serve on top.
4. To take things even further, garnish with thin apple crisps (see below).
5. Spike with vodka (optional).

Thin Apple Crisps
1. Thinly slice an apple into whole round discs.
2. Sprinkle icing sugar onto a baking tray lined with baking paper.
3. Then add the apple discs and sprinkle again with icing sugar.
4. Bake at 100C (215F) for 15-20 minutes.
5. Turn them over, sprinkle more icing sugar and bake for another 15 minutes.
6. Remove from oven and allow to cool.

These will store in the fridge for a good few weeks.

PORK, APPLE AND FENNEL SAUSAGE ROLLS

Shop bought, mass produced sausage rolls are a cheap treat. Homemade sausage rolls are awesome.

MAKES 12 ROLLS

- Splash of olive oil
- 3 cloves garlic, diced
- 4 rashers bacon, diced
- 1 bulb fennel, diced
- 1 apple, peeled and diced
- 10 sage leaves, sliced
- 2 tbsp parsley or thyme, chopped
- 1 tbsp fennel seeds, toasted and ground in the pestle and mortar
- ¼ tsp grated nutmeg
- Salt and pepper
- 500g (1 lb) pork mince
- 100g (1¼ cups) fresh breadcrumbs
- 2 eggs
- 1 tbsp wholegrain mustard
- 500g (1 lb) ready made puff pastry
- 1 tbsp sesame seeds
- 1 egg, beaten with 2 tbsp of milk (egg wash)
- Flour to sprinkle

1. Put a frying pan on medium heat, add a slug of olive oil, the garlic and diced bacon, and fry it up a little.
2. Next add the fennel, the apple and green herbs. Stir in the fennel seeds, a little grating of nutmeg, salt and lots of black pepper.
3. Gently fry for around 5 minutes until everything is evenly cooked and aromatic. Set aside to cool.
4. In a large bowl mix the pork mince, fresh breadcrumbs, 2 eggs, mustard and the cooked apple fennel mix.
5. Roll up your sleeves, get your hands dirty and mix it really well. You are looking for a marvelously sticky, meaty mix.
6. Cut your pastry into 4 even sections
7. On a slightly floured surface, roll out each piece to form a rectangular shape (about 5mm in thickness) and brush with egg wash mix.
8. Place the meat on one side of the pastry and roll over the pastry to form the sausage shape. Keep it nice and tight and overlap the ends and pinch the pastry to seal in the meat – you should have a nice sausage shape.
9. Repeat the process with the 3 remaining pieces of pastry.
10. Transfer to a tray and refrigerate for 30 minutes to let things 'firm up'.
11. Once chilled, place on a chopping board and slice each into 3 (or more if you want).
12. Line 2 trays with baking paper and heat oven to 180C/ 350F.
13. Brush the egg wash mix on top of your sausage rolls and sprinkle with a few sesame seeds or fennels seeds, then bake for around 25 minutes until golden and all puffed up.
14. A top tip is to turn the trays halfway round for a even cooking
15. Uncooked sausage rolls can be frozen in sealed freezer bags for up to 3 months
16. There is no need to defrost these before cooking but allow an extra 10 minutes to cook through.

Eat with our homeamde apple mustard ketchup – you'll find the recipe on page 58.

SIMPLY SENSATIONAL SALMON TART

WITH FENNEL SLAW

Smoked salmon is an expensive treat and there never seems to be enough in the oversized packaging. So stretch it out by making a beautiful tart. I really recommend you make your own pastry, but shop bought is fine too.

For the filling:

- 400g (14oz) pastry, homemade is preferable
- 280ml (1 cup) single cream
- 3 eggs
- 1 lemon, zest only
- Salt and pepper
- 450g (1lb) new potatoes, cooked
- 150g (5oz) good quality smoked salmon
- 3 scallions, trimmed to finger length
- 1 tbsp capers, chopped

For the pastry:

- 300g (10.5oz) cold, salted butter
- 450g (1lb) plain flour
- 2 eggs
- 1 tbsp cold water
- Tart case or cake ring
- 500g (1lb 2oz) dry and cooked rice/dried beans/pulses/ baking beads
- Baking parchment

Pastry is easy to make, so we're including how to make your own in our recipe. If you're using shop bought pastry start on step 6.

1. Dice the cold butter and, using your fingers, work it into the flour to form a sand like texture. Keep a few lumps of butter; that makes for nice flakey bits.
2. Beat the 2 eggs and water in a teacup and add it to the flour and butter mix.
3. Work the mixture by hand until it forms a dough.
4. Toss onto a floured surface, bringing everything together and kneading it once or twice. The secret here is not to 'overwork' the dough.
5. Form it into a flat ball, wrap in cling film and chill it in the fridge for around 30 minutes.
6. Grab your cake ring or tart case, and rub a little butter onto the surface.
7. Roll out your pastry slightly bigger than your tin, to the thickness of your ear lobes. Pop it in the tin, pressing in the edges and forming a 1-inch lip to your tart.
8. Line baking parchment over the pastry and spread out baking beads or dry chickpeas to 'blind bake' your pastry at 170C (360F) for around 15 minutes. This prevents your crust going soggy when adding wet ingredients.
9. Take out just before the edges go golden and remove the paper and beads carefully.
10. Beat together the cream, eggs, lemon zest, salt and pepper.
11. Slice the cooked potatoes and arrange half of them on the pastry, then scatter the smoked salmon, pour on half of the egg mix, add the rest of the potatoes, scatter the capers, then pour on the remaining mix.
12. Give the tin a bit of a wobble and a tap so the mix fills in the gaps.
13. Arrange the scallions on top and bake for around 25-30 minutes at 170C (360F) until firm to the touch with a little bit of colour.
14. Once cooked, let it cool for around 15 minutes before trying to remove it from the tin.
15. The tart is best served at room temperature.

FENNEL SLAW

- 2 bulbs fennel, sliced as thinly as possible (I like to use a mandolin)
- 1 lemon, zest and juice
- 1 tbsp crème fraîche
- 1 tbsp horseradish sauce
- 2 tbsp pumpkin seeds
- 1 tbsp golden raisins (optional)

1. Mix all of the above in a large bowl.

Best served on a sunny Sunday afternoon for high tea with your Gran.

OPEN RYE NEW YORK STYLE SANDWICH

Nothing is better than putting in the time and effort to make a really good sandwich. The trick here is getting that bacon extra crispy and the eggs perfectly gooey.

SERVES 2

- 4 slices of awesome rye bread, toasted
- 4 eggs
- 4-6 slices of streaky bacon
- ½ avocado
- 1 tbsp sour cream or yoghurt
- Dash of Tabasco sauce or a pinch of cayenne
- Salt & pepper
- Squeeze of lemon
- Sprigs of frisée lettuce

I have chosen bitter frisée lettuce to cut through the richness of this dish; alternatively you could use bitter endive or go hipster with foraged dandelion leaves.

1. Heat the oven on high.
2. Line a baking tray with baking parchment and spread out your bacon nice and flat.
3. Line another piece of parchment on top of your bacon and lay down some sort of weight on top (e.g. a baking tray of similar size or clean brick).
4. Bake at 200C (400F) for 15-20 minutes. By baking the bacon between two sheets of parchment paper, the end result will be perfectly flat, crispy brown bacon. You can also fry the bacon with a weight on top.
5. Bring a small pot of water to the boil. Drop in the eggs for 4 minutes.
6. Remove the eggs and rinse under cold water to prevent any further cooking.
7. In a small bowl, smash up the peeled eggs with a fork. You want the runny yolk to almost form a mayonnaise.
8. Season with salt and pepper.
9. For the avocado dressing, blend together the avocado and sour cream with a dash of Tabasco, squeeze of lemon and a pinch of salt.

Next up, build the mighty sandwich!

1. Butter up your toasted rye bread and pour on your smashed eggs with a twist of the black stuff.
2. Top with frisée lettuce and balance shards of crispy bacon on top.
3. Drizzle avocado dressing all around.

Rye, you bacon me crazy!

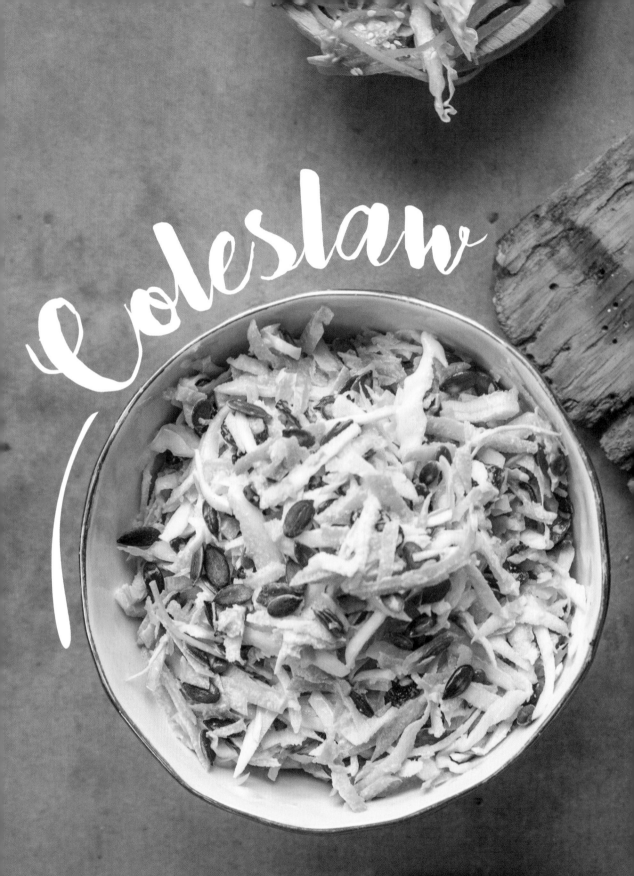

Coleslaw

...four ways

There is just so much more you can do with coleslaw.

The elements of good coleslaw are

TEXTURE, SWEETNESS, CREAMINESS and FLAVOUR

ASIAN SLAW

CELERIAC AND PUMPKIN SEED SLAW

Awesome with slow-cooked pork belly.

- ¼ Chinese cabbage (also known as Napa cabbage)
- 2 carrots
- 1 pak choi
- 6 sugar snap peas
- 2 tbsp salted peanuts
- 2 tbsp sweet chilli sauce
- 1 tbsp sesame oil
- 1 tbsp honey
- 2 limes, juiced
- Sesame seeds to garnish

1. Thinly slice all the vegetables into long sticks.
2. Chop the peanuts and stir into the vegetables.
3. In a separate bowl, whisk together the sweet chilli sauce, sesame oil, honey and lime juice.
4. We wait until serving time to dress this salad. The lime juice will make it appear dull and sludgy if added several hours in advance.
5. Finish with sesame seeds.

This goes amazingly well with duck or chicken. Celeriac is a root vegetable with a nutty flavour that is part of the celery family. It's really versatile and can be roasted or eaten raw.

- ½ celeriac
- ¼ white cabbage
- 3 carrots
- 4 tbsp mayonnaise
- 1 lemon, juiced
- 1 tbsp honey
- 3 tbsp pumpkin seeds
- 3 tbsp golden sultanas

1. Remove the outer skin of the celeriac.
2. Grate all the vegetables on the biggest setting.
3. Stir in mayonnaise, lemon juice and honey.
4. Fold in the seeds and sultanas.
5. Stir and enjoy.

RED CABBAGE SLAW WITH BEETS, APPLES AND CRANBERRIES

Goes down well with a nice cheese board.

- 2 beetroots, raw
- 2 apples
- ¼ red cabbage
- 2 tbsp yoghurt
- 3 tbsp dried cranberries
- 3 tbsp sunflower seeds/ crushed walnuts
- Twist of black pepper

1. Peel and grate the beetroot and apples.
2. Slice the red cabbage as thinly as possible.
3. Place in a large bowl and fold in the rest of the ingredients.
4. Add a twist of black pepper (optional).

TARTAR SLAW FOR FISH

Brings something extra to a fish dish.

- ¼ white cabbage
- 3 carrots
- 3 tbsp mayonnaise
- 1 lemon, juice and zest
- Handful of dill, chopped
- 3 medium gherkins, diced
- 1 tbsp capers

1. Slice the white cabbage thinly.
2. Grate the carrots.
3. Add chopped dill, lemon juice and zest to the mayonnaise.
4. Stir in the gherkins and capers.
5. Fold into the vegetables.

INDULGENT CHICKEN LIVER PÂTÉ

Pâté sounds fancy and difficult to make, or perhaps a little off-putting because you're not used to handling internal meat organs. Don't fret, it's not only easy to make, it's actually hard to get wrong. Liver is also very good for you, although liver pâté is a little indulgent.

MAKES 6-8 PORTIONS

- 150g (5oz) butter (at room temp)
- 2 shallots, finely chopped
- 600g (1.5lbs) chicken livers
- 1 tsp thyme leaves
- 1 tsp tarragon or parsley, chopped
- 2 tbsp brandy
- 1 orange, juice (optional) or if you have orange liqueur even better
- 125ml (½ cup) cream
- Salt & pepper to season
- 150g clarified butter (*make this at the end to pour over the finished pâté)

To serve

- 8-10 slices of white bread (the cheap, nasty stuff)
- 4 tbsp good quality marmalade
- 1 orange, zest and juice
- 2 tbsp of brandy
- 1 tsp dark brown sugar, optional

1. Melt 50g of butter in a large frying pan until it begins to foam.
2. Add the shallots and cook for around 5 minutes until soft.
3. Next add the livers and herbs and cook on a medium heat until they are slightly brown on the outside and a little pink in the middle.
4. Add in the brandy (or orange liqueur), flambé it if you wish, to cook out the alcohol (tip the pan to one side, light the liquid and it should flame for 30 seconds or so).
5. Add in the juice of one orange.
6. Take off the heat and let it all rest for 5 minutes or so.
7. Blend the mixture in a food processor or with a hand blender, slowly adding in the cream and the remaining butter (not the clarified butter).
8. Process until smooth, taste and season with salt and pepper.
9. Divide into ramekins or even use china teacups.
10. Spoon on the clarified butter to form a seal, this will lock in the flavours, and help preserve the pâté.
11. Refrigerate.

To serve it up:
1. Preheat the oven to 160C/315F.
2. Remove the crusts from your slices of bread and roll as flat as possible with a rolling pin, to get them extra thin.
3. Cut into triangles and bake for around 5 minutes until golden and crisp, then cool on wire racks.
4. Gently warm up your marmalade in a pot and fold in a dash of brandy, zest of one orange and a teaspoon of dark brown sugar (optional).
5. Serve on wooden boards with a baby leaf, hazelnut and orange salad.

* To make the clarified butter:
1. Melt butter in a pot.
2. Separate golden oil (95%) from the white whey (5%).
3. The golden oil is the clarified butter - pour this on top of the finished pâté pots and discard the white liquid.

Sea
Swimming

Sea swimming, or wild swimming, has taken the world by storm. A dip in the big blue is not only invigorating fun, it also helps to boost your immune system and mental wellbeing. There are two levels of saltwater swimming: The first is simply getting your gang together for a spot of jumping off the rocks (be careful) and having a splash in ocean. The next level is where you swim from cove to cove and get a few kilometres under your belt, for which you might join a group or set yourself a goal like an open-water race.

To get started, there are a few factors to consider.

Know before you go
Check the tides, swell, currents, weather and water conditions. (For example, if there's been heavy rain there could be toxic runoff in the sea.) Always scout the area, both on land and what lies beneath the water. If you're doing a longer swim, be sure you've got a few exit spots so you can get out at any stage if need be.

Safety first
Always hit the water with a swim buddy. It's never a bad idea to do a rescue or basic first aid/ CPR course to feel more confident and deal with problems or panics that could arise. Go online and learn the 'frog jump', which ensures you enter the water safely. Never dive! When you're rock jumping, every rock and barnacle will feel extra-sharp; there's no shame in wearing shoes. And if you know there are jellyfish about, pack a bottle of vinegar to deal with stings.

Creature comforts
Post-swim gear is essential to get your body back up to temperature. Even if it's a hot day, have a dry bag with a towel, bobble hat, warm footwear and dry clothes to change into. If you're planning on doing a long swim, pack a protein-based snack to help with recovery afterwards, plus a flask filled with soup, tea or coffee.

Scoping the sites
Check spots at high and low tides to see what you are swimming above or jumping into. Local swimming clubs often set up buoys out to sea, and these are useful if you'd like to set yourself a circuit or route.

Delightful dips

Dips aren't just an after thought – they add colour, flavour and texture to a dish. Plus, they are a great way to get extra veg into your meal. However, don't rely on ready-made dips, which come with added preservatives and hidden ingredients. Dips are usually quick and easy to make, and can transform a mediocre meal into something special. If you aren't that confident in the kitchen, dips are a good place to start being creative and getting into cooking a bit more. So give them a try!

BUTTERNUT & GOATS' CHEESE DIP

Another great way to get that veg into your diet; this delish dip is packed full of vitamin A. Wonderful to chomp down with a decent loaf of bread and a platter of cold meats, this is also good as a stuffing in chicken – or why not try stuffed mushrooms? You can even pimp it up at Christmas time by adding some chopped pecan nuts

For the dip

- 1 large/ 2 small butternut squash, peeled and diced
- 3 tbsp rapeseed oil
- 1 tbsp fennel seed (optional)
- 2 tbsp honey
- Rindless goats' cheese

For the caramelized onions

- 2 large white onions
- 2 tbsp olive oil
- 2 sprigs of thyme (save one for making the dip)
- 1 tbsp butter

1. Roast the butternut squash with the rapeseed oil and fennel seed at 190C (375F), until soft with crispy dark edges. This should take about 30 minutes.
2. Remove from the oven and drizzle with two tablespoons of honey.
3. Slice the onions and sauté in your heaviest frying pan, with olive oil and a few sprigs of thyme, stirring occasionally until they are soft and golden.
4. After the first few minutes add the knob of butter to help soften the onions. The onions will take longer than you think, keep stirring them on a medium heat for a good 20 minutes.
5. The secret to good caramelized onions is to scrape the bottom of the pan, getting all of that brown gooey stuff stirred through the onions. Once done place onto a chopping board and chop down into little pieces.
6. To combine, mash the butternut squash with a fork, fold in some good quality goats' cheese, the chopped onions and a few sprigs of fresh thyme leaves.
7. Taste and season with a pinch or two of salt, or perhaps some honey.
8. All this is possible with a food processor but by doing this by hand you get a better result and texture.

THE NOT
SO BORING
HUMMUS

Tired of eating hummus all the time? Then g
ive this roast garlic, parmesan and butter bean
dip a go.

- 3 garlic bulbs
- 3 tbsp olive oil
- 2 x 400g tins butter beans, drained
- Salt and pepper
- ½ lemon, juiced
- Sprig of fresh thyme
- Parmesan cheese, as much as you can afford, grated

1. Preheat your oven to 200C (400F).
2. Wrap each garlic bulb in foil with a splash of oil and roast for 30-35 minutes.
3. Remove from the oven, take out of the foil, slice one end and squeeze out the garlicky goo. Watch out, it will be hot.
4. In a food processor blend the butter beans, roasted garlicky goo, olive oil, salt, lemon juice and thyme until smooth.
5. Loosen the mix with a couple of teaspoons of water, add the grated parmesan and blend once more.
6. Taste and season accordingly.
7. Best served on an open roast chicken sandwich.

AROMATIC GREEN CHILLI SAUCE

This recipe is more than a dip – it's one of my all-time favourite recipes that goes with just about anything. You can rub it on meat as a marinade, you can serve it with crisps at a party or spread it on your favourite sandwich. Not for the faint-hearted, it's pretty spicy.

- 3 or 4 green cardamom pods
- 2 tsp cumin seeds
- 3 or 4 whole cloves
- 1 large bunch fresh coriander
- 1 large bunch fresh parsley
- 8 green chillies
- 2 tbsp oil
- Salt
- 1 lemon, juiced

1. Grab a pestle and mortar and bash the cardamom pods.
2. Remove the husks and keep the black seeds.
3. Keep bashing, adding the cumin seeds and whole cloves, grinding everything to a course powder.
4. In a food processor blend the coriander, parsley, chilli, oil, salt, lemon juice and crushed spices into a fine paste. You can add a tablespoon of water to adjust the consistency.

Job done!

BABA GANOUSH

For your next nosh!

Despite its cool name, people often turn their nose up when they hear this delicious dip is made with aubergines. Turn that frown upside down and give this classic recipe a go; hopefully it will change your attitude towards aubergines for good.

SERVES 4

- 4 aubergines
- 2 garlic cloves, crushed
- 2 tbsp tahini paste
- 1 lemon, juiced
- 2 tsp cumin seeds, save some for sprinkling at the end
- 1 tsp toasted coriander seeds
- Salt and pepper
- Parsley, chopped
- 1 tbsp olive oil

1. Pop your grill on high. Now burn your aubergines. Yes, that's right, blacken that skin. Turn them around for an even burning. This should take around 10-15 minutes. I like to handle mine with BBQ tongs.
2. Once cooled, scoop out the flesh and chop it down a little with a sprinkling of salt.
3. Pop the aubergines into a colander and let them drain for a good 20 minutes. This is an important stage as the liquid that strains away holds a lot of bitterness.
4. Tip the aubergines into a food processor and add the garlic, tahini, lemon juice, toasted spices and plenty of salt and pepper, then whizz up to a purée.
5. Taste and season; you should get a lovely smoky flavour coming through.
6. Serve with scattered chopped parsley, a trickle of olive oil and a sprinkle of cumin.
7. This goes down well stuffed into pita pockets with lamb, chicken or a meaty fish.

RUBY
DELIGHT DIP

With it's bright colour, incredible nutritional value and versatility, beetroot is an exciting culinary adventure. With this recipe we bake the beetroot. These beets will nut be beaten!

Before the invention of tin foil, salt baking was all the rage. Lucky for us, these days tin foil pretty much does the same job as the traditional salted pastry method.

- 3 large beetroots,
- ½ cup walnuts, lightly toasted in a hot dry pan for two minutes, save some to garnish
- 2 tbsp dill, chopped
- 2 tbsp crème fraîche, save some to garnish
- 1 tbsp balsamic vinegar
- 1 tsp toasted caraway seeds (optional), save some to garnish
- Salt and pepper
- Splash of olive oil
- Dill

1. Toss the beets with olive oil and a very generous sprinkling of salt in a large bowl.
2. Individually wrap each one with foil and bake for around 90 minutes (depending on the size) at 200C (400F). When you test the beets with a sharp knife, it should easily pierce through the centre.
3. Cool, unwrap and gently rinse in a colander.
4. Whizz the beets, walnut, dill, crème fraîche, vinegar and caraway seeds in a food processor until smooth. Remember to save some of the ingredients to sprinkle on top at the end.
5. Taste and season with salt and pepper.
6. Serve in a bowl topped with crème fraîche, caraway seeds, sprig of dill, crushed walnuts and a drizzle of olive oil to keep its shine.

This is great served on dark brown bread with smoked mackerel and a pint of Guinness.

BIG
BOLD SALADS

Don't think of salads as just garnish or a bit of limp greenery on the side. Things are changing. We are becoming less reliant on a meat-and-veg type of dinner and actively trying to introduce more raw food into our diet. Our salads are flavoursome and hearty enough to be a main meal – not just an afterthought. A proper salad should have:

FLAVOUR · TEXTURE · COLOUR

Each forkful should give a different sensation and a different concentration of each salad element.

Generally speaking, these salads combine starch, protein and fresh seasonal veg. We have included some pulses too, to give an alternative to the common carbs like potato and breads. By adding some protein such as eggs and cheese, it adds extra weight to the salad, transforming it into a solid meal.

I love using vegetables in salads – especially as we are used to boiling veg to death. In these salads we hold their character by just lightly cooking and adding beautiful flavours to enhance their presence.

The beauty of salads is that the variations are endless. If you don't like goats' cheese, switch to blue cheese. Try a nut oil for a change and see how it brings out different flavours. Start to play with combinations and textures by adding nuts or seeds for extra crunch.

Just have fun with them and try to incorporate one of these awesome salads into your weekly meal plan. Your

MEXICAN-STYLE PRAWN, CORN AND AVOCADO SALAD WITH CORIANDER

Chopped salads are a new trend on the high street. Everything is chopped down and mixed together well, making super-tasty salads that are easy to eat and a great way to get your kids into salads, too.

The best way to go about making chopped salads is to use a very large chopping board and a big, sharp knife. Crispy lettuce leaves like romaine, iceberg or endive make really good chopped salads. Some say less is better, but for chopped salads, the more the merrier. Give this this Mexican-style prawn, corn and avocado salad a go.

SERVES 4-6

- 4 corn on the cob – you can use tinned but the whole corn is better
- 400g (12oz) cooked and peeled prawn tails
- 1 tbsp garlic butter
- Flat leaf parsley, chopped
- 2 heads of romaine lettuce
- 1 red pepper
- 100g (3.5oz) cherry tomatoes
- 2 sticks celery
- ¼ red cabbage
- 1 fennel bulb
- 1 red onion
- 1 chilli
- Bunch of spring onions
- 1 bunch of coriander
- 1 handful of baby spinach
- 1 carrot, grated
- 2 avocados

For the dressing:

- 2 limes, juice and zest
- 2 tsp sugar
- 100ml (⅓ cup) olive oil
- ½ tsp cumin

1. For an extra awesome salad, start by cooking the corn on the cob in a pot of boiling water for around 5 minutes, then drain and finish off in a frying pan with BBQ seasoning and butter, allowing it to burn on one side.
2. Slice down the cob to get the big juicy bits of corn with a slight caramel texture to them.
3. Next pan fry the prawns with some garlic butter, finish with chopped flat leaf parsley and set aside to cool.
4. Chop down all the ingredients separately: The romaine leaves are done coarsely; the red peppers, tomatoes, and celery are chopped finely; the cabbage, fennel and carrot are thinly sliced.
5. Start adding everything together with the remaining ingredients. Keep stirring and fold in your corn and prawns, toss around, mix and chop, chop, chop. If you feel like a pro you can use two knives.
6. I like to add my avocados last so they don't turn to mush.
7. In a cup blend together the lime, sugar, olive oil and cumin to make the dressing to pour over your salad
8. Serve the salad with warm flat bread, a wedge of lime and a sprig of coriander.

GASTRONOMIC DELIGHTS

ONCE WE HIT THE ROAD ALONG THE ATLANTIC COAST OF FRANCE AND DOWN TO SPAIN – WHICH IS PROBABLY ONE OF THE MOST STUNNING, GASTRONOMIC SURF TRIPS YOU COULD EVER DO. If there's any place where food and surf culture meet head-to-head, this is it. We picked up a van in Bordeaux, the epicentre of wine, and went to Cap Ferret, the oyster capital of Europe. From there we headed to Biarritz and carried on into San Sebastian, a Basque town with some of the best restaurants in the world.

Walking down the street with a surfboard under your arm in a buzzing town like Biarritz or San Sebastian is quite a different experience to Irish surfing, which tends to be more about wild corners than cities. The waves aren't exactly beginner-friendly in France – there are a lot of heavy beach breaks, with things mellowing out a bit once you hit Spain. The surfing beaches are quite spread out so you can pick and choose your spots, or you can go up into the Pyrenees if you fancy some adventure away from the ocean.

Punctuated with pintxos, shellfish and wine, this trip provided the perfect combination of beach life, culture, surf and food.

LENTIL TABBOULEH
AND DUCK CONFIT

Tabbouleh is a traditional Lebanese salad made with bulgar wheat and parsley. Here we have substituted the bulgar wheat with lentils, which make a great accompaniment to duck. Jane and I had a similar dish down in South West France when we were surfing. This is the perfect grub to feed a hungry soul after some sandy barrels.

SERVES 4

- 250g (1¼ cups) puy lentils
- 1 bunch spring onions
- 200g (7oz) cherry tomatoes
- 1 very large bunch flat-leaf parsley
- ½ red onion, finely chopped
- Large bunch mint
- Olive oil
- ½ lemon, juice and zest
- Salt and pepper
- 2 large or 4 small portions of duck confit (traditionally the legs and thigh meats are confit). I sometimes use a tinned version and that is totally fine.
- Large bunch of watercress
- Dollop of crème fraîche

1. Rinse the lentils and bring to the boil in plenty of salted water for 25-30 mins (until tender) or as per packet instructions.
2. Drain and set aside to cool.
3. Drizzle the lentils with a little olive oil and a sprinkle of salt.
4. Finely slice the spring onions and quarter the cherry tomatoes.
5. Chop down the parsley as finely as possible.
6. Pick the mint leaves and chop them down.
7. Combine everything together, add in the onions and mix with the lentils in a large bowl. Add a splash more olive oil, the juice and zest of one lemon, salt and pepper, and serve at room temperature.
8. Cook or warm through your duck confit as per packet instructions, pull the meat off the bone and divide into four portions.
9. Serve each portion in a nice bowl piled high with tabbouleh salad. Sit the shredded duck on top with a large sprig of watercress and a dollop of crème fraîche.
10. Sprinkle cracked black pepper from a height like a pro.

Grab your favourite bottle of classic Bordeaux red wine and tuck in with a crunchy French baguette.

GRILLED ASPARAGUS CAESAR SALAD

Ah yes, the Caesar salad, as common as spaghetti bolognaise. So let's twist it up a little, ditch the romaine lettuce and add in grilled asparagus. YEAH!

SERVES 2

- 2 bunches of asparagus
- 2 eggs, soft boiled and peeled
- 4 rashers of streaky bacon, sliced into pieces
- 1 wedge of parmesan cheese
- Caesar salad dressing
- Knob of butter
- Salt and pepper
- Anchovies (optional)

1. Grab a steak skillet or the thickest pan you have and get it scorching hot.
2. Throw down your asparagus and let it burn on one side a little.
3. Turn down the heat, toss the asparagus, throw in the bacon and let it fry away.
4. Finish with a knob of butter and twist of salt and pepper.
5. Assemble with sliced soft egg, lashings of parmesan cheese (I like to use a vegetable peeler), a drizzle of Caesar dressing and delicately placed anchovies.

GREEN BEAN AND NEW POTATO SALAD

WITH HALLOUMI AND DILL YOGHURNAISE

Yoghurnaise? What's that? I hear you say. Well it's my awesome, tangy mixture of thick, herby yoghurt and mayonnaise.

SERVES 4

- 600-700g (1.5lb) new potatoes
- 7 garlic cloves (5 for the potatoes, 2 for the green beans)
- Drizzle of olive oil
- Salt and pepper
- 400g (1lb) green beans
- 225g (8oz) pack of halloumi cheese
- Dash of white wine vinegar
- 1 large bunch flat-leaf parsley, chopped
- 1 lemon, juice and zest
- Salt and pepper
- Sprig of dill

For the dressing:

- 3 tbsp Greek-style yoghurt
- 1 garlic clove, grated
- 1 large bunch dill, chopped
- 2 tbsp thick mayonnaise
- Twist of black pepper

1. Preheat the oven to 200C (400F).
2. Cut the potatoes into quarters or small chunks and put them into a large roasting tray with 5 smashed garlic cloves.
3. Add a good dash of olive oil, salt and pepper, toss the potatoes around and roast for 45 minutes, giving them a stir halfway through.
4. While the potatoes are roasting, steam or boil the green beans and leave them to one side to cool down.
5. Pop a pan onto a high heat, add a dash of oil and pan fry thick slices of halloumi cheese, turning them after 30 seconds. You are looking for a nice salty, crispy colour to your cheese. Remove from the pan but keep the pan hot and perhaps add another splash of oil.
6. Add 2 grated garlic cloves with the cooked beans and give them all a quick toss in the pan.
7. Add a splash of white wine vinegar or balsamic vinegar and let them sizzle for 30 seconds, coating the beans in a nice, garlicky vinegar.
8. Remove potatoes from the oven, squash the roasted garlic, throw in the beans, chopped flat-leaf parsley and squeeze of lemon juice, and give it all a good toss to get everything to marry.
9. In a separate bowl, add chopped dill, a grated garlic clove, yoghurt, mayonnaise and perhaps a twist of pepper, and mix well.
10. Serve your potato bean salad in a large open bowl with the fried halloumi and a good dollop of herby yoghurnaise on top.
11. Finish with the lemon zest and a sprig of dill.

This goes down well with grilled chicken or a spring lamb chop, and perhaps a glass of Pinot Noir or Portuguese Albariño.

SO-CAL CULTURE

WHEN WE LIVED IN SAN DIEGO WE HAD THE FANTASTIC OPPORTUNITY TO EXPLORE THE IDENTITY AND CUISINE OF THE USA'S WEST COAST, WHICH FEELS QUITE DIFFERENT FROM THE REST OF AMERICA. As well as a huge Mexican influence and a great sense of health and well-being, it also seems like there's a lot of fun to the foodie scene in California – with social group eating, casual dining done really well and feel-good comfort food.

Californian culture supports lots of farmers' markets and small producers, which means high quality ingredients are really accessible. You also get organic supermarkets in California – not just an aisle or a section, but the whole store. You can go in with a big trolley and shop 100% organic, often in bulk and with paper packaging. It's great to spend time in a population that's so environmentally aware and cares about the provenance of its food.

In terms of surf, Southern California is the land of the party wave. The climate is great so you can hang out at the beach all day and jump in for a wave or two, unlike in Ireland where surfing is more of a mission. It might not have the best waves in the world, but California has got some of the best road trip possibilities and tons of variation. You can find spots for bodysurfing, logging, high-performance shortboarding, big waves, competition surfing – in California anything goes!

GREEN PEPPER SALSA

We tried this Green Pepper Salsa when we were living in California and it transformed our meals. We've been serving it at home ever since, and it's great seeing people's reaction as green pepper isn't always everyone's favourite vegetable. However, this little mix elevates the humble green pepper to the next level.

Great served over a chicken breast.

SERVES 4-6.

- 2-3 green peppers
- 2 tomatoes, de-seeded
- 1 red onion
- 2 cloves garlic
- 2 green chillies, de-seeded if you don't like heat
- 1 lime, juiced
- Salt and black pepper
- Fresh coriander
- 3-4 tbsp olive oil

1. Grab a pair of BBQ tongs and burn the peppers on the open gas hob flame. If you don't have a gas hob, get your hands on a blow torch and go all Hollywood flame-throwing style.
2. Once the skin on the peppers is burnt, scrape away, leaving a nice green flesh.
3. Finely chop the peppers, tomato, onion, garlic and chillies.
4. Add a pinch of salt, a squeeze of lime juice and a twist of pepper.
5. Stir through the olive oil to bind everything together.

AMAZING FISH TACOS

INSPIRED BY SO-CAL CULTURE · SOUTHERN CALIFORNIA

When it comes to tacos, most people think of the hard-shell, corn chip supermarket tacos. Although tasty, these are a more American version. The original tacos are in a soft, round flat bread made from masa. These are easy to make, but it's difficult to source the ingredient.

Instead you can make them with a small, soft, wheat-flour tortilla, but keep an eye out for the real thing in speciality shops.

So you have your soft flour tortillas.

There are 6 elements to this recipe, which should make around 8 tacos.
1. Pickled red onion
2. Hot mayonnaise
3. Corn relish
4. Fish
5. Garnish
6. Tortilla

PICKLED RED ONION

- 2 red onions
- 4 tbsp red wine vinegar
- 1 tbsp sugar
- 4 tbsp warm water

1. Slice the onions as thinly as possible.
2. Add the rest of the ingredients and allow to pickle (from 15 minutes to a whole day).

CORN RELISH

- 1 tin sweetcorn
- 1 fresh red chilli, finely chopped
- 3 tbsp coriander, chopped
- 1 tsp sunflower oil (to bind)
- Pinch salt
- Pinch ground cumin

1. Mix altogether and put to one side.

HOT MAYO

- 6 tbsp mayo
- 2 tbsp good hot sauce
- 1 tsp honey

1. In a bowl, stir all the ingredients together.

FISH

- 4 large white fish fillets, like hake, haddock or monkfish tails, sliced into bite-size pieces
- 2 tsp ground cumin
- 1 tsp smoked paprika
- 3 cloves garlic, grated
- 3 tbsp sunflower oil
- Salt & pepper

1. Place the fish in a bowl.
2. Toss with the spices, herbs and 1 tbsp of oil.
3. Drizzle the rest of the oil on a baking sheet.
4. Add the seasoned fish to the baking sheet and cook for around 15 minutes at 180C (375F).

TO SERVE

- ½ red cabbage, thinly sliced
- 3 limes
- Bunch of coriander

1. Warm the tortillas in a hot dry pan and place under a cloth to keep the heat in.
2. Have all the ingredients lined up and let's build these tacos.
3. Start with the flatbread.
4. Sprinkle on the red cabbage.
5. Spoon on the fish.
6. Followed by corn relish.
7. And a squeeze of hot mayonnaise.
8. Finish with pickled onion, fresh coriander and a slice of lime.

Tuck in! These go down well at sunset with some chilled Mexican beers.

BIG WAVE SURFER BARRY MOTTERSHEAD'S PASSION FOR OUTDOOR LIVING IS INFECTIOUS. HE LIVES A SIMPLE, AUTHENTIC LIFE THAT IS ENRICHED BY NATURE AND THE EXPERIENCES HE CREATES FROM IT. BARRY IS THE KIND OF PERSON WHO COULD BE DROPPED IN A JUNGLE OR A FOREST AND SURVIVE HAPPILY FOR WEEKS ON END. IN FACT, HE PROBABLY WOULDN'T EVEN WANT TO BE RESCUED!

WILD AT HEART

Wild camping isn't only about getting away to the middle of nowhere. Adventure starts at home. Before you commit to a month-long solo hiking and camping trip, why not just try camping out under the stars for a night within easy reach of your house?

UNDERCOVER

Consider the weather: do you even need a tent? If so, please don't buy a cheap one that's essentially disposable. Festival culture has flooded the market – and environment – with some really flimsy, terrible equipment. If you're going to dabble in camping, borrow a high-quality tent before buying a bad one. At the very least, you want good zips and fire-resistant qualities.

BAG IT UP

Again, there are lots of cheap, sub-standard sleeping bags out there, which will make your wild camping unpleasant. Our personal sleeping bags can handle temperatures that plummet to minus 15 degrees. Ok, we don't really need that for Ireland, but it means we can be really confident that we'll be comfortable when we're sleeping outside.

CREATURE COMFORTS

Just because you're camping, it doesn't mean you have to be a martyr to the elements. There's a lot more to life than sitting in a clammy tent with a packet of biscuits wishing the night away. Put some effort in at home with your prep: marinate the meat, pack spices, bring popcorn kernels and remember to bring a midnight snack like a bar of dark chocolate.

SLOW DOWN

Remember, you can camp out anywhere – it could be as simple as asking a farmer if you could pitch up on a hill in the farm for a night. Appreciate the view, your company and the conversation, and relish the opportunity for a digital detox. If you've ever wanted to try your hand at whittling, now's your chance. And if you're feeling brave, work a skinny dip into your slow-paced itinerary.

WILD CAMPING KIT

Bring matches (or a flint and steel if you fancy trying a bit of bush craft), dry clothes, talcum powder (for a dry shower), a mat to keep you off the ground, something for breakfast and a rubbish bag. Leave absolutely no trace – not even a single square of toilet paper or an apple core!

HAZELNUT LAMB KOFTAS
WITH A BROAD BEAN AND FETA SALAD

A little bit hipster but so cool if you make these on foraged sticks. I pick mine from a hazelwood tree, give them a clean and trim the tops with a veggie peeler. It's worth the effort.

SERVES 2-4

- 40g (½ cup) breadcrumbs
- 2 tbsp milk
- 600g (1.3oz) minced lamb
- 50g (¼ cup) hazelnuts (blended into crumbs)
- 2 cloves garlic, grated
- 1 tsp ground cumin
- 1 tsp ground coriander
- 2 tbsp rosemary, chopped
- Salt
- 1 egg

For the salad
- 1 baby cos lettuce
- 1 tin broad beans, drained
- 60g (½ cup) black pitted olives
- ½ cucumber
- ½ red chilli, diced
- 200g (7oz) feta cheese, chopped into chunks
- 1 lemon, zest and juice
- Olive oil
- Salt and pepper

1. Place the breadcrumbs and milk in a bowl and let the milk soak into the bread to soften.
2. Add the lamb, blended hazelnuts, garlic, cumin, coriander, rosemary, pinch of salt and the egg.
3. Using your hands, work the mixture until well combined and you can shape it.
4. Grab your sticks and form the meat around them into koftas (a long, skewered meatball shape).
5. Refrigerate for 20 minutes to let them firm up.
6. To prevent them from sticking to the BBQ, brush with a little olive oil.
7. Cook over medium-heat coals on a griddle, or pan fry them over the fire in an iron skillet with a splash of olive oil.
8. Build the salad with lettuce, butter beans, olives, cucumber, chilli and chunks of feta.
9. Make a simple dressing of olive oil and lemon juice (2 parts oil to 1 part lemon juice) and sprinkle the zest of the lemon over the salad.

I like to serve mine with warm pitta pockets and garlicky tzatziki.

sweet treats

THE QUEEN OF CAKES

Move over carrot cake! Honey and parsnip make a great combination when roasted together... so why not try them baked together? This Honey Parsnip Cake goes perfectly with a rich Assam tea or chai latte.

- 4 large eggs
- 200ml (1 cup) sunflower oil
- 125g (⅔ cup) light brown sugar
- 100g (5 tbsp) honey
- 250g (9oz) grated parsnip
- 100g (1 cup) desiccated coconut
- 300g (2½ cups) self-raising flour
- ½ tsp baking soda
- ½ tsp nutmeg (optional)

For the frosting

- 350g (12.5oz) cream cheese
- 2 tbsp honey
- 3 tbsp large flaked coconut

1. Preheat oven to 180C (360F), grease up a cake tin and line with baking parchment.
2. Beat the eggs, oil, sugar and honey in a bowl.
3. Stir in the grated parsnip and desiccated coconut.
4. Sieve the flour and baking soda into the mix and fold to form a batter.
5. Sprinkle in the nutmeg and mix.
6. Spoon into the tin and bake for around 40 minutes, until golden and firm to the touch.
7. Push a skewer into the centre of the cake and if it comes out clean, it's cooked. If it's still wet, bake for a further 10 minutes and test again.
8. Take out of the oven and allow to cool for a few minutes, then transfer onto a wire rack and allow to cool completely.
9. Keep the oven on to toast the flaked coconut to decorate. Put the coconut flakes onto a tray and bake for around 5 minutes until golden brown. Watch out – they burn quickly.
10. To make the icing, beat the honey and cream cheese together and spread onto the cooled cake.
11. Finish with toasted coconut flakes.

Serve with a rich Assam tea or chai latte.

THE
SIMPLE
LIFE

WE LOVE THE SIMPLICITY OF PORTUGUESE FOOD. IT GOES HAND-IN-HAND WITH THE LANDSCAPE – IT SEEMS QUITE RUSTIC AND THEN YOU GET THESE BEAUTIFUL PIECES OF DESIGN EMERGING FROM THE ENVIRONMENT.

And of course, in Portugal the surf pumps, too. It's quite different from the Irish surf scene, with a lot of heavy beach breaks. There's a really strong surf culture, but at the same time the beaches are so big you can get away from the crowds and get a peak to yourself.

Portugal is great for its little beach hut cafés where you can relax after the morning's surf and tuck into boiled octopus, grilled sardines or chicken piri piri, with a beer or a glass of Portuguese wine. It's not about sophisticated kitchens. A lot of the cooking is done over charcoal, and the result is cheap, cheerful and delicious dishes.

Pastéis de nata (Portuguese custard tarts) are almost a rite of passage for travellers here – the minute you get off the plane you're stuffing your face with them. The whole time you're in Portugal, you're going to have them every day for breakfast and snacks – you'll even find yourself driving out of your way to hunt down the best ones as soon as they come out of the oven. They're so connected to the surf lifestyle that we do them every Friday in Shells, and all the local surfers pop in for a fix.

PASTÉIS DE NATA

These divine Portuguese custard tarts are a must-try when on surf trips in Portugal. In fact, most people go to great lengths to hunt down the best version and will travel to find their favourite one. Although more of a dessert, when on a surf trip, these are a perfectly acceptable breakfast or pre-surf snack.

After so many surf trips to Portugal, our addiction to pastéis de nata grew and grew, so we decided to put them on the cake counter every Friday in Shells.

MAKES 24 (AND YOU WILL EAT THEM ALL)

- 1 sheet puff pastry
- Knob of butter to grease tray
- 350ml (1¾ cups) whole milk + 25ml (1/8 cup) for the roux
- 1 lemon, zest, but use a vegetable peeler for a wide cut
- 1 cinnamon stick
- 55g (½ cup) plain flour
- 315g (1⅔ cups) caster sugar
- 150ml (⅔ cup) water
- 5 egg yolks

1. Take the sheet of puff pastry and roll it lengthwise to form a snail shape.
2. Once rolled, cut into 1cm-thick discs.
3. Roll out each disc to the width of a muffin tray case.
4. Grease the muffin tray and line each mould with a pastry disc.
5. Place in the fridge to firm up while you make the custard filling.

Filling:
1. For the filling, put the caster sugar and water into a pot, bring to boil and simmer for a good 10 minutes. Then remove from the heat and allow to cool. This is the stock syrup.
2. In another pot bring to the boil the 350ml milk, lemon zest and the cinnamon stick.
3. Meanwhile combine the 25ml cold milk with the plain flour and mix to a smooth paste. This is the base for the roux.
4. Once the milk has come to the boil, strain it onto the roux, stirring to remove lumps.
5. Place this mixture back on a low heat and cook until thickened.
6. Once thickened, take the stock syrup and slowly incorporate the two together.
7. Blend this with a hand blender to remove lumps.
8. Strain and chill until cold.
9. Once the liquid is chilled, whisk in the egg yolks

Now you are ready to fill your tart cases.

1. Preheat oven to 260F (510F).
2. Fill each pastry case to ⅔ full.
3. Place tarts into the oven and reduce temperature to 240C (480F).
4. Bake for 15-20 minutes or until golden brown. The tarts like a high heat and are traditionally a bit burnt on top.
5. Remove from baking tray immediately after baking as they have a tendency to stick to the tray once cooled.

Enjoy any time of day with a coffee.

GARDEN THERAPY

Through her company, Space to Grow, Sophie Skinner supplies flowers to Shells. She grows her crop according to organic standards and these beautiful blooms travel less than a kilometre from the soil to our café tables. Her workshops – from wreath making to flower crowns – are always a hit at Shells. The flowers and foliage always look great – and they're proven to make you feel good, too!

"My family were all gardeners back in the day. Almost a decade ago I studied organic horticulture because I just knew I wanted to grow things and be outside. Now a lot of my work is social gardening – which is gardening with groups where the focus is more on the people than on the produce. A lot of this garden therapy is for adults who are being rehabilitated after injury, and children with learning and behavioural difficulties.

Everybody knows the colour green is relaxing. As well as creating space for social interaction and bringing the community together, gardening is great for de-stressing and promoting mindfulness. One of our projects gathered over 400 kids in one polytunnel, and every child got to grow something. The teachers commented on the huge difference the project had on the children's behaviour.

As a spinoff to working in gardens growing food and flowers, I wondered: 'What am I going to do with all these flowers sitting around the place?' That's where the idea to make flower crowns came from. I love the idea of people interacting with plants, so for me it's a way to bring the outdoors to people. I do a lot of hen dos, so the girls will make their flower crowns and then go out clubbing. The flowers out-party the girls by the end – they're still looking fresh the next day!

Wherever life plants you, bloom with grace.

ORANGE PULP & POPPY SEED CAKE

You'd be surprised how many food products in your cupboard use orange pulp as a filler – it's great for thickening things up. Don't be put off using pulp – it's easy to make and the result is a lovely moist cake.

A gluten-free, dairy-free and guilt-free afternoon treat.

- 3 oranges, 1 juiced
- 6 eggs
- 250g (1¼ cups) caster sugar
- 1 tsp ground cinnamon
- 1 tbsp poppy seeds
- 250g (2 cups) ground almonds
- 1 tbsp gluten-free flour (you can use plain flour if you don't want the gluten-free version)
- 1 tsp baking powder
- 1 lemon, juiced
- 2 tbsp sugar
- Crème fraîche, to serve

1. Begin by boiling up 2 whole oranges for around 25 minutes. Keep them just submerged in a deep pot by placing a bowl on top to keep them under the water (so the bowl is sitting in the pot).
2. Discard the water half way through boiling and refill with fresh, hot water – this removes the bitterness out of the peel (as the oils go into the water). However, if you love a good bitter marmalade, you can skip this part and keep the water.
3. Remove the boiled oranges from the pot and blend the entire orange into a pulp using a food processor.
4. In a separate bowl beat the eggs and sugar together.
5. Add the orange pulp, cinnamon and poppy seeds.
6. Fold in the ground almonds, baking powder and flour, and mix well.
7. Pour into a well oiled and lined baking tin – use one of the springform ones so you can easily remove the cake at the end.
8. Bake for around 45 minutes at 170 C (370 F).
9. Check with a skewer – it should come out clean when dipped into the cake.
10. While the cake is baking, boil up the juice of 1 orange and 1 lemon with the 2 tbsp of sugar.
11. If you have one, place a cinnamon stick in the pot.
12. Boil for 3 minutes until slightly reduced.
13. Pour this syrup over the warm cake, remove from tin and enjoy with a blob of crème fraîche.

OH SO HEALTHY CARROT CAKE

We've all been told that carrot cake isn't actually that healthy as it's loaded with sugar and butter. So we played around with a few recipes and came up with this one. We've swapped a lot of the bad stuff for good stuff, but it's still satisfactorily naughty.

- 12 dates, pitted
- 2 ripe bananas
- 6 tbsp sunflower oil
- 3 eggs
- 120g (1 cup) wholewheat flour
- 1 tsp baking powder
- 1 tsp baking soda
- 2 tsp ground cinnamon
- ½ tsp nutmeg
- 3 cardamom pods, seeds removed and crushed between 2 spoons
- 4 carrots, grated
- 75g (½ cup) raisins
- 50g (½ cup) desiccated coconut
- 75g (½ cup) walnuts, chopped

For the frosting:
- 200g (7oz) light cream cheese
- 2 tbsp honey
- ½ lemon, juiced
- Toasted seeds to sprinkle

1. Preheat the oven to 170C (360F).
2. Blend the dates, bananas and oil into a thick cream.
3. Beat in the eggs.
4. Sieve together the flour, raising agents and spices in a separate bowl.
5. Fold into the egg and banana mix.
6. Add in the grated carrots, raisins, coconut and walnuts and give everything a good stir.
7. Pour into a well greased and lined baking tin.
8. Bake for about 40 minutes – or until a skewer pierced into the middle of the cake comes out clean.
9. Once cooked remove from the oven.
10. Allow to cool on a wire rack.
11. Beat the honey, lemon juice and light cream cheese to make the frosting.
12. Evenly spread onto the cake and sprinkle with lots of toasted seeds.

PARENTS' SURF SCHOOL

The progressive Sligo Surf Club is aiming to build one of the best community surf centres in Europe. Not long ago they started offering local children a free weekly surf lesson to help get the next generation surfing. But one condition was that a parent needed to accompany each child. It quickly came to light that some of the parents couldn't swim or were nervous in the water, and didn't want to transfer their fear onto their children.

We swiftly realised that we needed to get the parents surfing too, so Shells came on board to sponsor a weekly session for the parents. Surfing's a part of our life, so it's lovely to share that passion. Now we see parents on the beach glowing with surfing stoke – and it's amazing to see the infectious love of the wave-riding spread throughout our community. It all just goes to show that it's never too late to change your life a little bit, and to experience that raw happiness that being outside in nature gives you.

COCONUT MACAROONS

These are great little treat that have some health benefits and aren't too fattening! We love to make these macaroons for the parents and kids at the surf school.

MAKES 12-15

- 190g egg whites (4 or 5 eggs, yolks removed)
- 250g (1¼ cups) sugar
- 250g (2½ cups) desiccated coconut
- 50g (⅜ cup) plain flour
- 50g (2oz) crushed raspberries
- 1 lime, zest
- Dark chocolate to garnish

1. Combine all the dry ingredients.
2. In a separate bowl whisk the egg whites until they become frothy (it doesn't need to be stiff), then combine the egg whites with the dry ingredients.
3. Add your flavour of choice – we love lime and raspberry, as above.
4. With wet hands form egged-shaped balls and place onto a baking tray lined with parchment paper.
5. Bake in the oven at 160C (340F) for 15-20 minutes or until golden brown.
6. Garnish with melted dark chocolate.

Other awesome flavours to try include:
- Lime zest and mint
- Candied ginger and dried pear
- Dried cranberry and orange zest
- Dried apricot and lemon zest
- Strawberry and basil

RETRO RICE KRISPIE SQUARES

Nothing says old skool like this original recipe from a 1970s Rice Krispie packet.

• 150g Rice Krispies

• 4 tbsp golden syrup

• 1 tbsp sugar

• 1 tbsp butter

• A few drops of vanilla or almond essence

1. Put the syrup, sugar and butter into a pan.
2. Melt and bring to the boil for 1 min, stirring.
3. Remove from the heat, add vanilla essence and Rice Krispies.
4. Mix well, pour into a greased 20cm square tin and mark into squares. Alternatively, divide mixture between 12 cake cases in a baking tin.
5. Put in the fridge to set.
6. These delish treats will keep for a few days in an airtight tub.

SALTY STICKY CARAMEL KRISPIE SQUARES

Want to pimp-up your Krispie treats? These bad boys literally take about 10 minutes, so give them a try.

• 85g marshmallows

• Sprinkle of coarse salt

• 150g butter, in cubes

• 120g Rice Krispies

• Few drops of vanilla essence

1. Start by melting the butter in a pan and allow it to go a golden brown, then keep cooking until it smells fragrant and caramelly.
2. Reduce the heat and add the marshmallows until they are melting and all gooey.
3. Remove from the heat and stir in the salt, vanilla and Krispies.
4. Mix well, pour into a greased 20cm square tin and mark into squares. Alternatively, divide mixture between 12 cake cases in a baking tin.
5. Put in the fridge to set.
6. These will keep for a few days in an airtight tub.

CHOCOLATE CARAMEL KRISPIE SQUARES

Super-easy to make, I absolutely love these chocolatey, gooey Rice Krispie treats.

• 4 Mars Bars, roughly chopped

• 150g butter, cubed

• 120g Rice Krispies

• 150g milk chocolate

1. Grease and line a 20cm square baking tin with parchment paper.
2. Place the Mars Bars and butter in a heatproof bowl and place over a pan of barely simmering water.
3. Mixing with a whisk, melt until the mixture is smooth.
4. Put the Rice Krispies in a mixing bowl and pour the mixture over, stirring until all the ingredients are evenly combined.
5. Press evenly into the prepared baking tin and set aside.
6. Melt the milk chocolate in the microwave or over a pan of barely simmering water.
7. Spread the melted chocolate over the Rice Krispie mixture and leave to set in a cool, dark place.
8. Once set, slice into squares and serve!

ELDERFLOWER AND RASPBERRY CAKE

INSPIRED BY DERVLA CONLON · PUDDING ROW

Jane and I often struggle to find great places to go to on our days off, so when Dervla Conlon opened Pudding Row in Easkey it was a little slice of heaven on our remote coastline. I cheffed with Dervla in Dublin, where we made a strong connection because we share the same ethos and I just love her style. Just like at Shells, at Pudding Row all the breads and cakes are made in house.

Here is Dervla's Elderflower and Raspberry Cake recipe, so you can bring some of her west coast heaven into your home.

SERVES 8-10

- 135g (5oz) butter (room temperature)
- 200g (1 cup) vanilla sugar
- 4 eggs (separate yolks and whites)
- 1 whole egg
- 250g (2 cups) ground almonds
- 1 lemon, zested (reserve the juice for the glaze)
- 1 large punnet of raspberries
- 1 handful of flaked almonds

For the elderflower glaze:

- 2 tbsp lemon juice
- 75g (⅓ cup) caster sugar
- 100ml (½ cup) elderflower cordial (homemade is best)

1. Line a 22cm round, loose-bottomed cake tin with baking parchment and lightly coat the inside with odourless oil.
2. Preheat the oven to 180C.
3. Using a mixer, cream the butter and sugar together until it has turned completely pale, light and soft. This will take 10 minutes minimum.
4. Scrape down the sides of the mixing bowl with a spatula.
5. Separate the egg yolks and set the whites aside for whisking.
6. Add the whole egg to the butter and sugar mixture first, to loosen it, and then add the egg yolks one by one. Stop and start the mixer with each addition, scraping down once or twice in between.
7. Add the ground almonds and zest, and combine well with a spatula.
8. In a separate bowl, whisk the egg whites until they form lovely, soft peaks.
9. Carefully fold through the above mixture in two additions. Be light as a feather – this makes all the difference and will ensure the cake remains soft and light, instead of heavy and dense.
10. Pour the cake mixture into the prepared tin and dot the raspberries throughout it, pressing them in with your finger. I leave a few close to the top to add a little burst of colour to the golden cake.
11. Sprinkle with flaked almonds.
12. Bake at 180C for 35-45 minutes.
13. While the cake is baking, prepare your glaze. Combine the ingredients in a small saucepan and gently bring to the boil, then remove from the heat.
14. Once the cake is perfectly baked, the sides should be golden brown and a skewer should come out clean when inserted into the centre.
15. Remove from the oven and brush with the glaze while the cake is still in its tin.
16. Leave the cake in the tin until it is completely cool. Then, remove from the tin, place on a beautiful cake stand, dust with icing sugar and serve with a little crème fraîche or freshly whipped cream.

Enjoy with your friends and family.

DELICIOUSLY DECADENT DOUGHNUTS

Back on trend, doughnuts can be super simple or gourmet. They're a bit of an effort to make, but wow – what a treat!

- 400g (3¼ cups) plain flour
- 27g (⅕ cup) dried yeast
- 40g (¼ cup) caster sugar, plus extra to garnish
- 200ml (1 cup) full fat milk, room temp
- Pinch of salt
- 1 egg, whole
- 1 egg, yolk
- 45g (1.5oz) butter, room temperature
- 2 litres (8 cups) vegetable oil
- 150g (5oz) raspberry jam
- Rubber gloves (optional)

1. Measure the flour into a bowl.
2. Add yeast and sugar.
3. Stir and mix in all the dry ingredients.
4. Pour in the milk (if the milk is too cold, it won't activate the yeast – 30 seconds in the microwave should get it to the right temperature).
5. Get your hands dirty and mix it around to form a stiff dough. Push and pull the dough (kneading) in the bowl.
6. Add the egg yolk, egg, salt and butter as you knead, working the ingredients into the dough. It's pretty sticky, so I like to use rubber gloves when I do this.
7. Turn the mix onto a lightly floured surface.
8. Keep the surface well dusted with flour and keep kneading for around 10 minutes, until you get a nice shiny elastic dough.
9. Pop it back into the bowl, cover with a damp cloth or plastic shopping bag and allow to prove for 30/40 minutes. Place the bowl in a nice warm part of the kitchen, not by a cold breezy open window.
10. Again, turn out onto a floured surface and punch/knead the dough a few times over.
11. Roll out 10-16 'balls', depending on the size of doughnut you like.
12. Place them onto a flour dusted tray and allow to 'reprove' for about 20-30 minutes. They should grow to twice their size, so make sure to leave a large gap between them.
13. Ready to fry. Heat a deep pot with oil, to around 170C (340F). If you don't have a thermometer to test the temperature, a small piece of dough should rapidly boil and go golden within a minute.
14. Cook the dough balls in stages, don't overcrowd the pot. Allow the doughnuts to float and bob around for 3 minutes on each side. The bigger the doughnut 'balls' the longer the cooking time. A big mistake people make is undercooking doughnuts, so if in doubt break one open to check. If the doughnuts are going a dark brown, lower the heat of the oil.
15. Lift out with a slotted spoon onto kitchen paper, to soak up excess oil, then transfer onto a wire cooling wrack and allow to rest.
16. Poke a hole in the size with a chopstick and squirt in your favorite jam (mine's raspberry) using a piping bag or an old sauce bottle (with nozzle). I have even used my kids' medicine syringe!
17. Roll in caster sugar and indulge – go on, you deserve it!

CHOCOLATE VEGAN
ICE CREAM

This oh-so-simple recipe tastes amazing and even sneaks in some greens!

Most people don't try their hand at making ice cream because they think you need an ice cream maker. Well, you don't. And our no-churn chocolate ice cream proves you can get all the richness, flavour and creaminess of the real thing, with no ice cream maker required.

- 2 tins coconut milk
- 4 tbsp raw cacao powder
- 1 tbsp maple syrup
- 1 avocado, stone and skin removed (adds creaminess and thickness)

1. If you have a NutriBullet or blender, pop everything in and blend on high.
2. Pop into a tub and freeze.
3. A couple of times during the freezing process, stir through with a fork to help break down any ice crystals.
4. Once it's frozen, grab a spoon and tuck in!

Dinner

-Chicken-

Pig

Cow

KNOW YOUR *meats*

In the amount of time it's taken for the population of the world to double, meat consumption has gone up fivefold. These days cheap meat is too readily available and we're seeing negative environmental and health effects. It's getting out of hand. There's such an abundance of cheap meat that before you know it you're having it three times a day – along with the antibiotics, additives and hormones that intensive farming often requires.

Making conscious choices that are good for you and the planet means eating less meat, and eating better quality when you do. That means organic and local. Visiting Sri Lanka and India was a real eye opener for us. The cuisine features less meat than our typical Western diet, but you don't miss it because there's so much flavour, spice and colour. The richness and variety of the food means that you stop needing meat at every mealtime; then, when you do have meat, you really appreciate it.

BEATEN BLACKENED
PORK SHOULDER STEAKS
WITH WALDORF SALAD

A lean white meat, pork can be a little dry on its own, but magic with a few herbs and spices. The secret here is to rub on the spices and let things marinate for a couple of days.

SERVES 2

- Pork shoulder steaks
- 1 tsp cayenne spice
- 1 tsp ground coriander
- 1 tsp ground cumin
- 1 tsp dried oregano
- 1 tsp smoked sweet paprika
- ½ tsp salt

1. Blend the spices together and massage into your steaks.
2. Pop them, unwrapped, into the fridge for a day or two.
3. Get the pan on extra hot heat, add a splash of oil and sizzle your steaks to your liking.

WALDORF SALAD
WITH CROZIER BLUE

Crozier Blue is a creamy, mild blue cheese made from sheeps' milk. If you can't find Crozier substitute with any good quality creamy, mild blue cheese.

- 1 head romaine or cos lettuce
- 50g (½ cup) walnuts (lightly toasted in a dry pan)
- 1 apple or pear, diced
- Small handful grapes, halved
- 2 sticks celery
- 2 tbsp mayonnaise or yoghurt (if you want to be healthy)
- 2 tbsp of Crozier Blue, broken down into chunks
- Fresh tarragon (optional)

1. Slice the lettuce into bite-size chunks, add the walnuts, diced fruit and celery, and stir in the mayonnaise.
2. Top with Crozier Blue and tarragon.
3. Serve with your pork steak and glass of good Riesling.

HEALTHIER BANGERS
AND MASH

Sometimes we need comfort food, but we don't
need the guilt. Here we swap the potatoes for
cauliflower in the mash, choose a leaner sausage
and make gravy without frying the onions in
butter. Much healthier, yet just as delicious.

SERVES 2

- 1 cauliflower
- 1 tsp butter
- Salt and pepper
- Scratching of nutmeg
- 4 red onions
- 1 tsp tomato purée
- 1 tsp balsamic vinegar
- 1 tsp soy sauce
- 6 alternative sausages such a veggie sausages, turkey
  sausages, lean beef sausages or Quorn sausages.
  You can even go as far as asking your local butcher to
  make some sausages with less fat – it is easy for them
  to do.
- 1 sprig thyme

1. To make the mash bring your cauliflower to the boil, cook until soft
   and drain. Then blend with a stick blender, adding in a teaspoon of
   butter, salt, pepper and a scratching of nutmeg. A top tip is to let the
   cauliflower drain really well to get that mashed potato consistency.
2. Slice the onions and gently fry up in a pan, adding the tomato purée,
   vinegar, a couple of tablespoons of water and soy sauce. Stir and let
   the ingredients marry in the pan.
3. Pop the pan into the oven at 200C (400F) for 20 minutes and roast.
   Roasting the onions when making gravy is much healthier than frying.
4. While the oven is on, pop the sausages under the grill rather than
   frying.
5. Assemble on a nice wide bowl: a big helping of cauliflower mash,
   carefully balanced sausages and a generous spoonful of roasted
   onion gravy,
6. Garnish with a sprig of thyme.

Tuck in with less guilt.

SWEET, STICKY CHICKEN THIGHS ON PEANUT RICE NOODLES

I love this dish and I'm not the only one. I served it to a friend and ever since he keeps asking me for more 'chicken crack'. So be warned, this is seriously addictive chicken.

SERVES 2-4

- 6 chicken thighs
- Splash of oil
- 1 packet rice noodles
- 2 tbsp peanuts, chopped
- 1 tsp sesame oil
- 1 tbsp sesame seeds
- 4 scallions, chopped, to serve
- 1 tbsp sweet chilli sauce
- 1 lime, to serve
- Coriander, to serve
- 1 tbsp sweet chilli sauce

For the marinade

- 4 tbsp sweet chilli sauce
- 4 tbsp light soy sauce
- 2 limes, juiced
- 2 tbsp honey
- Thumb of ginger
- 3 cloves garlic
- 1 or 2 red chillies
- Splash sesame oil or peanut oil

1. Blend the marinade ingredients together and pour over the chicken thighs.
2. Allow to marinate for a few hours, giving them a gentle stir to ensure they are evenly covered.
3. Once the chicken has been well marinated, grab a nice thick pan, add a splash of oil and sear the chicken to give it some colour on both sides.
4. Transfer to a preheated oven at 200C (400F) and bake for 15-25 minutes, depending on the size of the thighs. Baste the chicken halfway through the cooking process.
5. Cook the noodles according to packet instructions, then toss in a little sesame oil and add the sesame seeds, chopped peanuts and sweet chill sauce.
6. Serve with fresh coriander, chilli and lime wedges, and top with chopped scallions.

GOOD OLD
steak
& salad

My top tips for steak:

1: There is only one type of steak that is worth eating and that is a rib-eye steak (if you must a sirloin or T-bone will do).

2: Buy from a butcher, and ask for the longest-hanging piece of meat they have.

3: Unpack your steak and let it sit on a baking tray or wire cooling rack in your fridge – let it shrivel and go dark, this is a good thing.

4: Take it out of the fridge a couple of hours before you are going to cook it. Never cook a steak from cold.

5: Salt both sides heavily at least one hour before cooking.

6: Get the pan as hot as you can – smoking hot (have the fire brigade on speed dial).

7: Cook it for exactly half the cooking time on each side, and let it rest on the chopping board for twice as long afterwards. For example, a total of 4 minutes cooking time would mean 2 minutes on each side and 8 minutes resting time afterwards.

BABY SPINACH AND RIB-EYE STEAK SALAD

Carb-free and delicious, steak and salad is the healthier choice.

SERVES 2

- 2 decent rib-eye steaks
- 1 medium squash, like butternut or pumpkin, skin on
- 1 red onion
- 1 tbsp honey
- 1 tsp cumin seed
- 1 tsp coriander seed
- 1 tsp fennel seed
- 1 tsp pumpkin seed
- Olive oil
- 2 large handfuls of baby leaf spinach
- Balsamic vinegar
- 100g (3.5oz) creamy goats' cheese – we love Bluebell Farm goats' cheese
- Handful of walnuts, crushed, to serve
- Salt and pepper

The secret to this salad is to keep the slices of squash on the larger side and with their skin on. Most people think the skin is inedible, but when roasted it adds a lovely sweet and nutty texture to the squash.

1. Slice the onion and butternut squash into large chunks and place in a baking tray.
2. Add the spices and pumpkin seeds, a dash of olive oil and a drizzle of honey.
3. Give everything a good stir so it all gets evenly coated.
4. Bake for around 20-30 minutes at 200C (400F) until golden and soft. Perhaps give everything a stir halfway through and add another drizzle of honey.
5. Cook the steak to your liking in a very hot pan, and do not forget to let it rest on a chopping board.
6. Grab a bowl and toss the spinach leaves with a drizzle of olive oil and a splash of good balsamic vinegar.
7. Assemble your salad with chunks of goats' cheese, strips of steak, roasted squash and onions.
8. Top with crushed walnuts.
9. Sprinkle salt from a height like a pro (sprinkling from a height actually gives everything an even coating).

Sit back, crack open an alcoholic ginger beer or a spicy Shiraz.

CHICKEN *wings*

Grab your bib and let's get cooking! These are great for a party – and who doesn't love wings? We've got two recipes we love to roll out – Sweet & Spicy or Crunchy Buttermilk.

SWEET & SPICY WINGS

Here's our take on the classic chicken wings recipe.

SERVES 4

- 1.8 kg (4lbs) chicken wings, tips discarded
- 350ml (1½ cups) fiery hot sauce – the hotter the better
- 175g (¾ cup) butter
- 300g (1 cup) runny honey
- 40g (2 tbsp) brown sugar
- 2 cloves garlic, finely diced
- 1 tsp cayenne pepper
- Salt and pepper
- 1 lime, juiced

1. Preheat the oven to 180C (350F) and grease the base of a large casserole or roasting dish.
2. Place the chicken in the dish and sprinkle with salt and pepper.
3. Bake uncovered for about 45 minutes, turning the chicken halfway through.
4. Combine the hot sauce, butter, honey, sugar, garlic, salt, cayenne pepper and a pinch of freshly ground black pepper in a medium sized pan.
5. Place over a low heat and melt the butter, stirring well.
6. Increase the heat and bring to the boil, continuing to stir.
7. Allow to cook for 40-45 minutes, stirring occasionally. The sauce will thicken to a syrupy consistency and reduce by half.
8. Have a taste and add a squeeze of lime juice.
9. When the chicken is cooked and the juices run clear, remove from the oven and drain off any cooking juices
10. Pour half the sauce into the dish and toss the chicken.
11. Return to the oven for a further 5 minutes, or at this point you can pop them under the grill or on the BBQ.
12. To serve, pour the remaining sauce over them.

Tuck in and get messy!

CRUNCHY BUTTERMILK WINGS

The best fried chicken always involves buttermilk – it not only gives a certain tang to the chicken, it also tenderises it. Win Wing! (Get it?!) Tip – it's best to marinate these the day before you need them.

SERVES 4

• 3 eggs

• 500ml (2 cups) buttermilk

• 1.8kg (4lbs) chicken wings, tips removed

• 400g (3 cups) plain flour

• 60g (1 cup) cornflakes, crushed

• Dried thyme

• ½ tsp cayenne pepper

• 1 tsp salt

• 2 cloves garlic, grated

• 2 litres vegetable oil for frying

1. Beat the eggs and buttermilk together in a large bowl until smooth.
2. Mix in the chicken wings, cover and refrigerate for a day (or at least an hour).
3. When you're ready to start the cooking process, preheat the oven to 220C (425F) and line 2 or 3 baking sheets/ trays with either foil or parchment paper.
4. In a large bowl, combine the flour and cornflakes with the pepper, thyme, cayenne, salt and garlic.
5. Remove the chicken wings from the buttermilk marinade and allow the excess batter to drip from the wings.
6. Press the wings into the crumbs and arrange on the baking sheets/ trays.
7. Bake for around 25-35 minutes, until golden brown and the juices run clear.
8. Preheat a pot of oil to 190C (375 F).
9. Fry the wings for a few minutes, in batches, to crisp them up.
10. Drain on a plate lined with paper towels and season with salt.
11. Serve up with your favourite dipping sauce.

THE MELTING POT

MYLES GREW UP IN SOUTH AFRICA; IT'S A WILD PLACE WITH A UNIQUE AND THRIVING FOOD CULTURE. WE LOVE TAKING FAMILY AND FRIENDS THERE FOR A PERSONAL INSIGHT INTO THIS AMAZING COUNTRY WHERE TWO OCEANS MEET. YOU GET REALLY INTERESTING SEA LIFE THERE – NOT JUST SHARKS, BUT LOTS OF TASTY FISH, TOO!

There's so much to do in South Africa that you could never, ever be bored. There's an abundance of waves, so there's always somewhere you can get waves to yourself. In a lot of places the landscape rolls straight from the beach into the mountains, because there's a whole mountain range that follows the coastline. It's one massive playground.

As well as diverse landscapes there's also a huge amount of wildlife. Not to mention the melting pot of cultures. In Cape Town there's a big Malaysian influence, while Natal has a huge Indian population and Johannesburg has been influenced by the Dutch.

In a sense it's quite unregulated; anyone and everyone can open up a shop. The result is that you get these amazingly creative spaces and an array of food options. It's really refreshing to tap into and it's never hard to find great wine, great food and great scenery.

South Africa has a huge farming industry and people really eat with the seasons. There's a great tradition of farm shops in South Africa, especially along the Garden Route. Farming cooperative stands – or Padstals – sell B-grade produce as well as homemade jams, preserves, biltong and homebakes. Some have really good reputations, so you'll drive hours out of your way to pop in for a visit. In South Africa, you'd do a road trip for the food alone, never mind getting to your destination!

KNOW HOW TO
barbecue

Lots of people think barbecue cooking is quite quick and easy, but it can also be a slow and delicate process.

Start with the best materials. Charcoal briquets are made of crushed charcoal powder and chemicals, which helps them light and hold the heat. However, lumpwood charcoal gives more flavour and imparts more of that essential smoky dimension. The latter is also more environmentally friendly. What we use is a blend of ash, beech, birch, oak, holly, blackthorn and sycamore, that's been locally sourced from sustainably managed woodlands and slowly fired in charcoal kilns.

When it comes to cooking on an open flame outside, it's all about heat control. Don't just light a fire, let it get hot and then throw everything on. Think about it the same way that you use a cooker and frying pan – you have to turn the heat up or down and shift your surfaces to get food closer to, or further away from, the source of the heat. In a barbecue setting, this means feeding or starving the fire and lowering or raising the grid.

Even with meticulous heat control, cooking over fire produces charring – and that's the whole point! The burnt bits lend a unique bitter dimension to the food. Traditional cooking offers a lot of salty, sweet and sour tastes, but it's rare that you get that satisfying bitter element.

Ultimately, this kind of cooking is primal; it's the most basic form of food preparation. But don't make the mistake of thinking that means it's just about meat. Vegetables cooked over a barbecue are beautiful – asparagus, corn on the cob, mushrooms and courgettes to name a few.

Somewhere deep down we're simply drawn to fire and cooking over the flames. It brings people together and is just about the most social form of cooking that exists.

SHOULDER OF LAMB
WITH HARISSA RUB

This awesome BBQ is guaranteed to impress your friends. There's a lot going on here, so read through the entire recipe a few days before your BBQ. Get yourself organised and GO FOR IT!

We'll be building two separate BBQs here – one for the veg and one for the meat. The veg take a lot of room on the fire and have to be close to the coals, which doesn't leave much room for the meat.

SHOULDER OF LAMB
WITH HARISSA RUB

- Shoulder of lamb, deboned (ask your local butcher to debone a shoulder of lamb, or even a leg of lamb.
- Garlic cloves
- Salt
- Ground cumin
- Harissa paste (shop bought or see page 48 for our homemade harissa paste).

1. Put your slab of lamb on a chopping board and – with the sharpest knife you've got – open it up into one long flat piece of meat.
2. Then slice down long perpendicular lines in one direction. This will open up the shoulder to help spread it out. You are looking for a flat layer of meat of even thickness
3. Give it a bash with a meat hammer (if you've got one) or a heavy, blunt object.
4. Cut away any sinew or silver skin.
5. Stab the meat with holes and stuff them with sliced garlic cloves.
6. Rub down the meat with salt and ground cumin, followed by a good massaging of harissa paste. Be sure to get it in all the nooks and crannies.
7. Do this in the morning and allow to marinate for a good few hours (in the fridge).

CHARCOAL BBQ VEG

You want hard, rooty vegetables for this one.

- Large butternut squash
- Hummus
- 4 beetroots
- 8 potatoes
- Salt
- Olive oil
- 1 celeriac, peeled
- Butter
- Thyme, fresh
- 4 onion
- Tin foil, lots of it

1. Grab the squash and trim the hard knob off the top (sometimes done already). With a large knife, split it in two halves – down the middle, then scoop out the seeds.
2. Spoon in the hummus.
3. Hold it together again and wrap three times in foil, nice and tight. Twist and turn the ends.
4. Pop the beetroot and potatoes in a large bowl with a generous sprinkle of salt and good glug of oil, and give them a toss.
5. Wrap each one individually in good quality foil.
6. Rub the celeriac with lots of butter, thyme and salt.
7. Wrap tightly in two layers of foil
8. Keep the skin on the onions, rub with oil and wrap in foil.

As well as your lamb and foil-wrapped veg, you'll need:
- Thinly sliced green veg
- Salt
- Lemon zest
- Olive oil

RIGHT, LET'S GET COOKING!

On the veg fire:

1. Once the charcoal on the fire has turned white, spread it out evenly.
2. Lay the foiled veg on top of the coals. The bigger, harder vegetables go in the middle and the softer ones (onions) go on the outside, where it's a bit cooler.
3. Turn every 15 minutes or so and give them a quick check about 30/40 minutes in.
4. Pierce with a sharp knife and when cooked it should cut through easily.
5. Cooking time depends on the thickness of the veg. On average they take about 40-50 minutes.

And the meat fire:

Ok, so the veggies are now on the go, let's get the lamb on.

1. Again you want an even layer of charcoal.
2. Place the BBQ grid 10/15cm above the fire. Sometimes propping with wood or rocks to get the right height. As the charcoal cools you can lower the grid closer to the coals.
3. If you are doing a big BBQ for a large group, you may need a 3rd fire on the go to feed the hot coals into the second fire (from the 3rd).
4. Place the meat on the grid.
5. Don't fuss over it – just leave it alone to cook.
6. If your fire begins to flame, it's too hot – you may need to raise the grid and splash a little water over the flames. You don't want flames!
7. Depending on the size of the meat it should take about 25 minutes of BBQ'ing.
8. Take some of the marinade and keep basting the lamb throughout. If you want to look like a real pro make a brush out of rosemary sticks.
9. Only turn 2 or 3 times, and perhaps more often towards the end of the cooking.
10. Don't be afraid to do a deep cut into the meat to see how pink it is. You can also press down and look at the juices – it shouldn't be bright red.
11. If you are struggling with time you can split the lamb in two to check it. Don't over cook it – a bit of pink is good.
12. Rest the lamb for a good 15 minutes before cutting.

To serve:

1. Carefully take out the veg, unwrap and add some nice flavoured butter to them.
2. While the lamb is resting, oil up some thin green veg, like asparagus or purple sprouting broccoli and lightly BBQ on the coals for a few minutes.
3. Serve with a sprinkling of salt, lemon zest and olive oil.
4. Slice the lamb.

What a feast!

BEER BEEF BRISKET
WITH ROASTED GARLIC MASH

Justin is our head chef at Shells, and the two things he loves best are BEER and COOKING. So it's no surprise that his favourite Beer Beef Brisket recipe sells out in no time when we put it on our specials board. This is a great one for entertaining – just make sure you keep a beer for yourself.

We love using beer from the White Hag brewery. The flavours are awesome and they are all brewed right here in Sligo. Try the Little Fawn Session IPA for a real malty flavour to the beef, or if you want something different use the Puca Berry Beer, which will add a certain tang and tartness to the dish.

For the beef:

• 1 tbsp olive oil

• 2 tbsp unsalted butter

• 1 large white onion

• 1.5kg (4lbs) beef brisket

• Salt and pepper

• 5 cloves garlic, peeled and smashed

• 350ml (1½ cups) beer or ale

• 2 tbsp Worcestershire sauce

• 2 tbsp balsamic vinegar

• ¼ tsp garlic powder

• ¼ tsp smoked paprika

For the mash:

• 900g (2lbs) floury potatoes, peeled

• 55g (2oz) butter

• 4 tbsp cream

• 4 tbsp flat parsley, chopped

• 1 bulb smoked garlic

• 2 tsp smoked paprika

• Sea salt and pepper to season

1. Add the oil, butter and onions to a skillet over medium heat.
2. Cook until lightly caramelized (about 15 minutes).
3. Remove from pan and set aside.
4. Liberally salt and pepper the brisket on all sides.
5. Sear the brisket in the onion pan until browned on all sides.
6. Place beef brisket in a roasting tin.
7. Top with the onions and garlic, then add the beer, Worcestershire sauce and balsamic.
8. Cook in oven at 200C (390F) and roast for 30 minutes.
9. Take out of oven turn the temperature down to 140C (285F), cover the meat with foil and return to the oven, for 4 hours (by which time it should be very tender).
10. While the beef is in the oven, roast the garlic bulbs in tin foil, with a drizzle of rapeseed oil and a pinch of salt and pepper to season.
11. Boil the potatoes until soft. Then add the butter and cream to the potatoes and mash.
12. Remove the garlic from tin foil and squeeze it out of its skin (use a hand towel). It should be a paste-like texture.
13. Add the roasted garlic paste to the potatoes and any juice from the tin foil for added flavour.
14. Mash again to ensure all ingredients are combined.
15. Add parsley, and season with salt and pepper.
16. Remove the brisket, thinly slice and top with onions and juice from the pan.
17. Serve with the garlic mash.

CRAFT BEERS

At Shells we love serving craft beer – it goes hand-in-hand with our ethos of small-batch production and amazing taste. We love to get away from the mass-produced brands and explore what people's imaginations are capable of. Sligo-based White Hag Brewing is always inventing new flavours, so we offer their seasonal specials at Shells and like to pair their unusual craft beers with our Supper Club menus. Here's what Joe Hearns at White Hag Brewing has to say about craft beers:

"I'm from Ohio but moved to Sligo over three years ago to become White Hag's Brewmaster. Craft beer is about creativity. I look at craft beer the same way I look at food. It's all about having variety. We make around 30 different beers at the moment, and soon we'll be making around 40.

Beer derives its flavour from four main ingredients: water, yeast, hops and grain. The art is the balance of each. When you look at music we only have 13 notes.

But how many songs have been written over the years using just those 13 notes? So while we have just four main ingredients, the possibilities are endless.

Interestingly, everything on one side of our building has been mainly influenced by my experience in the States, while everything on the other side is drawn almost completely from European influences. For example, we're aging some beer in French wine barrels, using Belgian style brewing and developing an apple-based ale that draws from the Italian grape ale tradition. My idea is to utilise the world's beer knowledge and bring it to Ireland.

Good craft brewing is more like the wine industry than the beer industry. In fact, craft beers have more characteristics than wine – such as dry, sweet, bitter, sour, malty and earthy. This means you can do more accurate food pairings with beers than you can with wines."

KNOW

MANY PEOPLE ARE DRAWN TO THE SEA, ESPECIALLY SURFERS. EVERY COASTLINE IS UNIQUE, AND YOU'VE GOT A WHOLE BIODIVERSITY OF MARINE LIFE WAITING IN EVERY COASTAL REGION YOU VISIT. SO THE NEXT TIME YOU'RE TRAVELLING, TAKE TIME TO GEN UP ON THE MARINE SYSTEM YOU'RE IN. WHETHER IT'S COLD, WARM OR TROPICAL, ALL WATER IS HOME TO MAGNIFICENT SEA LIFE.

When it comes to seafood, we've all got our favourites, from shrimps on the barbie to fresh sardines or fish and chips. But when you're travelling, stay true to the region you're in and eat what the locals eat – it's often quite different to what's served in the tourist restaurants. Local options will not only be fresh and delicious, they also have a smaller environmental impact in terms of the food miles they've travelled.

Try to eat shellfish whenever possible because there's no shortage of many of these species. When you're back at home you won't be able to source the likes of fresh octopus, mahi mahi (dolphinfish) or blue crab that you find on your travels. So keep an open mind when you scan restaurant menus and skip past the cod and hake to try something different!

As you travel, keep an eye out for some of these fresh alternatives:

Ling • Gurnard • Rockfish • Brill • Dab • Megrim

your FISH

Coley · Whiting · Pouting · Tusk

PANFRIED MACKEREL
WITH WASABI BEET SLAW

"What did sushi A say to sushi B?" Whaaat saaaa bi!" A simple, healthy dish with massive flavour.

SERVES 2

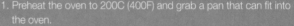

- 2 fresh mackerel, gutted and fins trimmed
- Splash of oil
- Any green herbs to stuff inside – like dill, parsley or tarragon
- 2 beetroots
- 2 tbsp crème fraîche
- 2 tsp wasabi
- 1 bunch of dill, chopped
- 1 tbsp of sunflower seeds
- 1 lemon
- 200g (1½ cups) boiled baby potatoes
- Handful of rocket

1. Preheat the oven to 200C (400F) and grab a pan that can fit into the oven.
2. Add a splash of oil into the hot pan and lay down the herb-stuffed fish for a minute or two, then carefully flip over with a spatula and pop it into the oven. Let the oven do the rest of the work for 10-15 minutes, depending on the size of your fish.
3. Meanwhile, get your potatoes on the boil.
4. Peel the beetroot and grate into a bowl (maybe put some gloves on for this).
5. Fold in 1tbsp of the of crème fraîche with the wasabi, chopped dill, sunflower seeds and a squeeze of lemon.
6. Taste and season with salt and pepper.
7. Drain the potatoes let them steam a little in the colander, cut them in half and toss them with a little butter and a sprinkle of sea salt.
8. To serve, place the fish on top of the boiled potatoes, pile on the beet slaw and another dollop of crème fraîche. Then add another squeeze of lemon, a drizzle of olive oil and sprinkling of sea salt.
9. Grab a handful of rocket leaves, gently roll them into a ball shape and delicately place on top.

Mackerel have way more flavour when they are cooked on the bone. The best way to eat them is to gently pull the meat off the bone with a fork.

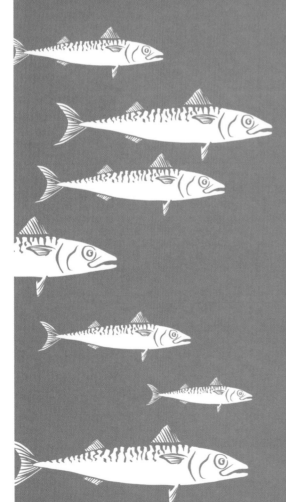

PEA AND TROUT SALAD
WITH PEARL BARLEY AND WATERCRESS

This is a lip-smacking Irish summer salad. Trout is a very sustainable fish, similar to salmon but with a slightly more earthy flavour. There are three major types of trout – rainbow trout, sea trout and brown trout. Here in Ireland we often surf at river mouths where we bump into a few fly fishermen and try to haggle a trout or two.

SERVES 2

• 2 fillets of trout, baked

Wrap the fillets in baking parchment or foil, with a drizzle olive oil, salt and pepper, and a squeeze of lemon juice or drop of white wine to help steam the fish, and bake for around 25 minutes at 180C (370F).

For the salad:
• 200g cooked peas
• 200g pearl barley, cooked as per packet instructions (I like to cook mine in a little bit of stock)
• 1 handful tarragon or dill, chopped
• 1 handful curly leaved parsley
• 2 lemons, zest
• 1 cucumber, peeled, seeds scooped out and sliced down into chunks
• 1 small packet of watercress

For the dressing:
• 3 tbsp rapeseed oil
• 1 tbsp lemon juice
• 2 tbsp horseradish sauce
• Salt and pepper

1. Combine all the ingredients for your dressing in an old jam jar and shake the hell out of it. Dressing done.
2. Grab a bowl, mix the cooked pearl barley, peas, green herbs, cucumber and lemon zest, to form the base of your salad.
3. To serve, pile the pea and pearl barley salad in the centre, flake your smoked trout on top and finish with a handful of watercress and a good drizzle of the dressing.

Washes down well with a wooded Chardonnay.

HOMEMADE FISH & CHIPS

Nothing beats home made: fresh fish coated in light, crispy batter with no additives. It's not exactly diet-friendly, but at least if you make it yourself you don't have to feel as guilty and you know exactly what fish is on your plate.

You'll need at least 3 litres of oil and a deep pot for this recipe. A chip cage or basket helps, but a slotted spoon will be fine.

FISH

Cod is the best – and most traditional fish to use – but that's the reason why cod stocks around the world are decimated. The good news is that they are slowly making a comeback. Hake, haddock, ling and plaice are a little more sustainable, but still under threat. Try to buy from an independent fishmonger and go for fish that has been caught by line and not by net.

BATTER

Chip shops lean towards a thicker batter as this helps keep their oil in good condition. However, a thinner batter will result in a crispier texture. Many pubs and restaurants use beer in the batter, but at Shells we use sparkling water as we feel it gives a really light and crispy batter.

To make the batter simply whisk together:

- 350g flour
- 500ml sparkling water
- Salt and pepper
- Dash of Tabasco

At shells we also sprinkle seaweed flakes into our batter.

DREDGING

Dredging is the process of dunking food in flour, then egg wash and then breadcrumbs. But for battered fish, you only need to dredge in seasoned flour and then into the batter.

1. In a deep pot, heat the oil to 190C, this will take at least 10 minutes.
2. Always keep an eye on a pot of hot oil in the kitchen – it's the primary source of kitchen fires. (If it happens to catch fire, do not throw water on it. Instead suffocate with a large towel.)
3. If you don't have a thermometer, test the temperature by dropping a teaspoon of batter in, and it should sizzle and boil straight way, then float to the top.
4. Pinch one end of the dredged fish and shake off any excess batter then slowly hold above the pot of hot oil.
5. Slowly dip half the fish fillet in and wave it around, along the length of the pot – doing this will create air pockets so the fish will float once you drop it all in (if you skip this part the fish will sink to the bottom). Let go of the entire fish into the oil.
6. Don't overcrowd the pot, only do 2 or 3 pieces at a time.
7. Cooking time will vary depending on the thickness of the fish. On average a 200g piece of fish will take about 4 minutes of frying time.
8. Shake the fish as you lift it, to get rid of excess oil and place on some paper towel.
9. Sprinkle with sea salt
10. Let the oil reheat and spoon out any excess batter bits before dropping another piece of fish in. You need to keep the oil nice and clean

TWICE-COOKED CHIPS

Maris Piper are the best spuds for chips – they also make delicious roasties.

1. Grab 2 potatoes per person.
2. Cut them as evenly as possible into long fingers – I like to keep the skin on for a more rustic feel.
3. Place them in hot oil for 2 or 3 minutes.
4. Take them out, allow to rest in a colander for around 5 minutes.
5. Repeat the process. This time placing on kitchen paper when you take them out.

Twice-cooked chips have a crispier skin and a fluffy centre. This fluffiness is down to the steam inside the chips while they are resting.

At Shells we serve them with a zingy lemon mayo. Boom! Job done.

seasoned flour

cover in batter

slowly dip and fry

yum...

ALTERNATIVE FRIES

THERE ARE POTATO FRIES AND THEN THERE ARE...

Carrot and parsnip fries
Polenta fries
Zucchini fries
Sweet potato fries

VEGETABLE FRIES

Veg fries are like french fries but made from other vegetables. They are very easy and very delicious. Are they healthier? Not really, but they're a little bit different from the norm.

- 5 carrots
- 5 parsnips
- 2 egg whites
- 4 tbsp Japanese panko breadcrumbs
- 1 tbsp of olive oil

1. Peel and cut your carrots and parsnips into chip-like batons.
2. Place the olive oil in a bowl and toss the veg into the bowl to coat evenly.
3. Fold in the beaten egg whites and panko breadcrumbs.
4. Spread onto baking sheets and bake at around 200C (400F) for 30-35 minutes until crisp and golden.

POLENTA SOLDIERS

- 400 ml (1½ cups) organic vegetable stock
- 150g (1 cup) quick-cook polenta, plus 2 tbsp for dusting
- 1 tsp butter
- 50 g (2oz) Parmesan cheese, plus extra to serve
- Olive oil

1. Bring the stock to the boil and slowly whisk in the polenta, stirring constantly with a wooden spoon.
2. Add a pinch of sea salt and butter, and after a few minutes, once thickened, finely grate in the parmesan.
3. Pour into a greased and lined 20cm square tin and pop in the fridge to chill and firm up (about 1 hour).
4. Preheat oven to 220C (425F).
5. Cut the chilled polenta into fingers and brush with olive oil.
6. Dust with the extra polenta and arrange on a greased baking tray in a single layer (make sure to leave spaces between each one) and bake for 30 minutes, or until crisp and golden.
7. Serve the hot polenta chips with some extra parmesan grated on top and one of our dips (see page 94) on the side.

ZUCCHINI FRIES

Although courgettes and zucchinis are the same vegetable, I think its Aussie name just sounds better than 'Courgette Fries'.

- 6 large zucchinis (courgettes)
- 1 litre (4 cups) vegetable oil, for frying
- 500ml (2 cups) cold milk (cold is important)
- 500g (2 cups) plain flour
- Sea salt crystals
- Cracked black pepper

1. Split the zucchinis lengthways into quarters and slice away the middle seeded part. Further slice down into thin strips of about 4mm in thickness.
2. Spread them out on a tray and sprinkle a little salt on them to draw out some of the bitterness.
3. In a large pot bring the oil up to 190C (375F). You can test the temperature with a small piece of bread, which should turn golden in a minute.
4. Dredge the zucchini in milk, toss in the seasoned flour, then place in the boiling hot vegetable oil carefully (don't overcrowd).
5. Cook for around 3 minutes.
6. Remove with a slotted spoon onto kitchen paper and sprinkle with salt.
7. Eat with spiced mayonnaise or salsa verde.

SWEET POTATO FRIES

WITH AVOCADO TAHINI DIP

This healthy summer feel-good snack goes fabulously with a BBQ

SERVES 4

- 4-5 large sweet potatoes
- Salt
- 3 tbsp olive oil
- Cumin seeds

For the tahini dressing:

- 1 avocado
- 3 tbsp of tahini (sesame paste)
- Fresh coriander (the bigger the bunch, the better)
- 1 lime, juice and zest
- 1 tbsp olive oil
- 1 garlic clove, grated
- ½ tsp cayenne pepper
- Salt

1. Preheat the oven to 200 (400F).
2. Wash and cut the sweet potatoes into long wedges.
3. Pop them into a bowl and add salt, cumin seeds and oil, and give them a good toss.
4. Pour them out onto a baking tray and pop into the oven.
5. Bake for around 25-30 minutes, giving them a turn once or twice for even cooking. You are looking for golden, crispy potato wedges.
6. For the dip, pop the avocado, tahini, coriander, lime juice and zest, one tbsp of olive oil, salt, garlic and cayenne pepper into a food processor and blitz until very smooth.

Dip away!

SUPER SHELLFISH

Loaded with good fats and iodine, shellfish such as oysters, clams and mussels feature frequently on the menu at Shells. You can do so much with them beyond just boiling or steaming – we'll never forget a smoked oyster roll we once had in California! You can pickle them, barbecue them or serve them cooked but cold – for example, try throwing mussels into a cold salad with fennel and smoked fish. These are underutilised and often underrated products, but so versatile.

As well as being good for you, many kinds of shellfish are truly abundant and sustainable. Raising shellfish is a very friendly form of farming. Except for scallops, which should be hand-dived, a lot of shellfish options represent relatively unprocessed farm-to-plate eating.

We recently served fresh oysters at a few festivals. We were been blown away by the number of people who had never had one. It became a challenge for people equivalent to doing a shot at the bar. Friends would get a round in and do countdowns as each one downed their oyster. It was cool to see people trying a natural food from our coast in a way that made it fun rather than aloof.

This kind of seafood is so impressive when you're entertaining too. Any time that you offer a big pile of shellfish there's always a wow factor: it's big and bold. There's also a communal angle, similar to eating chicken wings or ribs. Shellfish really is finger-licking, hands-on food that brings a crowd together.

OYSTERS

Oysters are simply amazing and packed with goodness. Full of vitamins, anti-inflammatory and antioxidant properties, they are also a really good source of B12, omega 2, iron and zinc. It's the high amount of zinc that makes them an aphrodisiac. Don't say we didn't warn you!

KNOW YOUR OYSTERS

Pacific Oysters: Small and sweet and the most cultivated/ farmed type of oysters, which makes them one of the most sustainable seafoods available.
Atlantic Oysters: Slightly rounder and more popular in the States, these are sometimes known as Blue Points.
European Flats: With smooth, flat shells and lovely seaweed and sharp mineral tastes, these wild, native oysters – also known as Belons – used to be the most common in Europe.

OYSTER ROCKEFELLER

Many restaurants around the world have their own style of Oyster Rockefeller – a dish that consists of oysters on half shells topped with yummy ingredients (usually green and herby), then baked or grilled. It's so rich and flavoursome that is it was named after Rockefeller, who was the richest person in the 1900s, when the dish became popular.

It's pretty impressive to serve your own style at a party – so give it a go. Here's our version:

LEEK AND CHEDDAR ROCKEFELLER

- 18 oysters, shucked
- ½ tbsp butter
- ½ leek, finely diced – as small as possible
- 1 tbsp (heaped) plain flour
- 1½ cups of milk
- 1 tbsp dijon mustard
- 100g (½ cup) vintage cheddar, grated
- Dill or seaweed to serve
- Pinch cayenne pepper

1. Place a small pot on a medium heat, ready to make a roux.
2. Melt the butter slowly.
3. Stir in the flour, using a wooden spoon to form a paste.
4. Slowly add in the milk and keep stirring until it starts to thicken.
5. Reduce the heat.
6. Add in the mustard, cheese and perhaps a pinch of salt.
7. Put a knob of butter in a separate small frying pan and fry up the diced leeks.
8. When the leeks are cooked, spoon in small amounts of the cheesy roux.
9. Spoon the cheesy leeks on top of the shucked oysters and pop under the grill on a high heat, until they begin to brown on top.
10. Serve with a sprig of dill or – even better – some seaweed.
11. Finish with a pinch of cayenne pepper.
12. Wash down with a chilled Chablis or Champagne – Rockefeller style!

Other Oyster Ideas
- **Oysters with Hot Mayo & seaweed.** Mix horseradish and wasabi with mayo and top with a little dillisk or sugar kelp
- **Oyster Mexicano -** with chipotle and grated tomato and coriander to garnish.
- **Oyster Avocado -** tabasco and avocado blended together and piled on top

MOY HILL COMMUNITY GARDEN, CO. CLARE

"If you do good things, good things will happen."

When you plant a tiny seed and cover it with earth, you never know just how big it will grow. The same thing happened to The Moy Hill Community Garden – it's an inspiration to us all. Pro surfer and Moy Hill Community Founder, Fergal Smith, explains how it happened.

A wise man once told me: "If you do good things, good things will happen." And not a word could be truer in describing the success of Moy Hill Community Garden.

A few years ago, a kind man generously gave us a small patch of land just outside of Lahinch in County Clare. It was matted with brambles and rushes, but with the help of a few friends and a hungry pig called Holly, bit by bit we began to clear it. It began to transform before our very eyes; people came and went, strangers became friends, and soon it became a beautiful garden full of flowers, vegetables and buzzing bees.

Today the community owns the garden and it's open to anyone and everyone – whether they want to plant a flower or simply sit on the bench and watch the world in Lahinch Bay go by. The garden's roots have grown deep within the local community, but this hasn't just happened by magic.

During the garden's first summer we held weekly cook-ups to share some of the fresh vegetables from the garden and meet other like-minded people. The next summer we were blown away by how many people came to the cook-ups – from grandchildren to grandparents. It was just incredible to see how this space could bring all different types of people together, and now we hold cook-ups every Friday from April until Halloween.

We are unique in that all of our work is done with a sustainable approach, as pigs help to rotavate the soil and we use local seaweed and sand instead of fertilisers or pesticides. We also work with several other non-profit organisations to promote healthy and sustainable communities in Ireland.

Anyone is invited to come and help us grow and, in return, when the harvest is done, is rewarded with the fruits and vegetables of their labour. Moy Hill has become a space where anything is possible – and this is what the garden has taught us.

So, if you are ever passing through County Clare on the Wild Atlantic Way, stop into the garden, make yourself a cuppa and enjoy the view.

www.growing.ie

DYNAMIC ROAST VEG

Tired of roasting the same veggies again and again?
Try these dairy-free, gluten-free, low-carb roasted
veg for a change.

SERVES 2-4 (2 AS A MAIN OR 4 AS A SIDE)

- 1 cauliflower
- 400g tin chickpeas, drained
- 2 chillies, diced
- 1 tsp smoked paprika
- 1 tsp curry powder
- 1 tsp cumin seed
- 1 tsp fennel seed
- ½ tsp ground turmeric
- 1 lemon
- Olive oil
- 5-6 kale leaves
- Salt

1. Preheat the oven to 200C (400F).
2. Chop the cauliflower into chunks and place on an oven tray.
3. Pour on the chickpeas and chopped chilli, and sprinkle with all of the herbs and spices.
4. Drizzle with olive oil and a squeeze of lemon (once the lemon is squeezed you can pop it into the tray with the vegetables).
5. Toss everything to give it a good coating.
6. Roast for around 25 minutes – giving it a stir a couple of times during the cooking process.
7. Five minutes before the end, coat the kale with olive oil and toss into the tray.

I like to eat mine with a dollop of yoghurt (or cashew cream if vegan) and some soft, warm flatbread.

EAT YER GREENS

You've probably heard that the mighty kale has been labelled the latest leafy superfood. Although it's easy to grow (especially in wet, cold climates like ours) and rich in nutrients, it can be a little bit difficult to eat. If you're still hesitant about cooking with kale, grow some of your own and embrace it. You can plant it in early summer and it grows all the way through to autumn – it's even hardy enough to handle a frost or two. Black kale – cavolo nero – is one of my favourites.

My top tips for kale-based salads:
- Always remove the ribs (stems) – the hardy centrepiece. Don't throw them away; you can mix them in with your dog food, or use in veg stock or in your next soup.
- Kale is usually quite a big leaf, so chop it down into small bite-size pieces.
- Pop the chopped kale into a bowl, sprinkle with salt and massage – this releases the fragrance, helps soften the tough leaf and makes it more palatable.
- Dress the kale before dressing the salad, to ensure an even coating on the leaves.
- Kales likes a fresh, zingy dressing.
- Don't serve a kale salad straight away – it needs to marinade first.

QUICK AND EASY
KALE SALAD

I make this using all homegrown ingredients

SERVES 2-4

- Large bunch of kale, stems removed and massaged in salt (see opposite)
- Salt
- 1 green apple
- 1 bulb fennel
- 100g (⅓ cup) goats' cheese (soft and creamy)
- Handful raisins (soaked in apple juice, if possible)
- Handful pumpkin seeds
- Handful pecans /walnuts, chopped
- 1 tsp caraway/ fennel seeds

For the dressing:

- 125 ml (½ cup) olive oil
- 1 lemon, juice and zest
- 1 tbsp honey/ maple syrup
- 1 tbsp Dijon mustard
- Pinch of salt
- Twist of pepper

1. Begin by prepping the kale: remove the stems, chop it down, massage in the salt and coat in a dash of olive oil.
2. Dice the green apple, keeping the skin on.
3. Thinly slice the fennel (as thin as you can get – I like to use a mandolin).
4. Make up the dressing by putting all the ingredients into a small bowl and whisking firmly with a fork.
5. Toss the dressing in with the kale and allow to marinate.
6. Get a hot, dry pan on the go. Toss in the caraway/ fennel seeds for one minute, followed by the nuts and pumpkins seeds, to heat through and slightly toast.
7. Fold into the kale mix.
8. Add in the juicy raisins. If you don't like raisins try dried cranberries or goji berries.
9. Plate up and sprinkle with goats' cheese and extra nuts and seeds.

STRANDHILL, COUNTY SLIGO.
IT'S SMALL BUT PERFECT
FOR OUR OUTDOORS
LIFESTYLE ON THE REMOTE
WEST COAST OF IRELAND.

MEET THE SHELLS TEAM

LUKE BALDWIN
BARISTA

Originally I'm from England but for the last seven years I've been living in Australia. I moved over here about a year ago because we met some friends in Perth who were from Sligo. Me and my wife were looking for a new adventure and we ended up just loving the place.

What's the best thing about Shells? Definitely the people. It's a very fun, laid-back workplace, and one of the best teams I've ever worked with. You can definitely have a good time!

If you could only eat one thing for the rest of your life what would you pick? I'm a chips fanatic. They're simple and essential. Around the world wherever I go, I have to get chips.

If you could fly anywhere right now where would you head to? I've been reading Che Guevara's The Motorcycle Diaries so I'd probably choose South America.

CHARUNAN BUNKHAN
ASSISTANT MANAGER

I'm from Thailand. My mother moved to Strandhill to work and she brought me with her, so now I've lived here for 11 years.

What's the best thing about Shells? The people! And the atmosphere – coming to the sea and looking at that view every day.

If you could only eat one thing for the rest of your life what would you pick? Rice – obviously. I'm Asian!

If you could fly anywhere right now where would you head to? Japan because of the food and new technology that they have. I've never been so I'm saving, saving....

HAZEL TELFORD
WAITRESS

I've been in Strandhill for two months. I'm from Sligo originally but was living in Australia for two years and then Indonesia for two years. My visa ran out, so I came back here and brought my boyfriend. He's Brazilian but I met him in Australia, and now he works in the Shells Little Shop!

What's the best thing about Shells? The people – we get lovely regulars who come in every day. It's nice to talk to them and see what's going on.

If you could only eat one thing for the rest of your life what would you pick? Pineapple.

If you could fly anywhere right now where would you head to? Back to Indonesia!

DIMITAR DOSER
BAKER

Originally from Bulgaria, I've been living in Strandhill for 16 years and working at Shells just under a year.

What's the best thing about Shells? The early mornings. As a baker I get to come in when there's no one around and see the sunrise. I like the serenity. As for the work, Shells is a great place that gives you the opportunity to create and try new things.

If you could only eat one thing

for the rest of your life what would you pick? Oysters!

If you could fly anywhere right now where would you head to? I've been to all the places I've wanted to go, so for me it would be a case of going back – and I would go back to French Polynesia just south of Hawaii. I spent a couple of months in the Society Islands. It's quite special.

LORNA GOLDEN
SHOP AND ADMIN MANAGER

I've been at Shells for two years. I'm from London and was a photographer there before moving over here about six years ago.

What's the best thing about Shells? The people, definitely. It's a really different bunch, both the regulars and the team. And it's a very positive, relaxed, supportive working environment, which is really nice.

If you could only eat one thing for the rest of your life what would you pick? Chips. I love chips so much.

If you could fly anywhere right

now where would you head to? If money was no object, I'd love a whole summer in Ibiza. A villa in the mountains, beautiful food, some yoga, swimming, a bit of clubbing. It's got the whole package – I love it.

WILL GAFFNEY
MANAGER

I'm from Sligo town and I came to work in Strandhill just over a year and a half ago.

What's the best thing about Shells? It's a really, really relaxed and laid-back environment. And I have a really good strong team.

If you could only eat one thing for the rest of your life what would you pick? Chicken burgers from Shells, which is all down to Myles and the chefs. It's probably one of the more popular things on the menu and unreal.

If you could fly anywhere right now where would you head to? Cancun, Mexico. I got married there and thought it would be a once in a lifetime thing. But I want to go back!

LISTINGS

If you're planning to visit this beautiful area, here's some information on places to stay, where to eat, which pubs to go to and interesting activities. This corner of Ireland will enchant you, so come here soon and set your spirit free!

ACCOMMODATION

By The Sea B&B
This family-run B&B offers a home-away-from-home ambience, private parking and wifi. In a quiet and secluded location in Strandhill village, it's only steps away from sandy beaches, fine dining and endless possibilities for recreation and relaxation.
Address: Burma Road, Strandhill, Co. Sligo
Web: www.bytheseastrandhill.com
Email: info@strandhillbytheseabandb@gmail.com

Strandhill Beachfront Apartment
Located right above Shells bakery and café, this is a one-bedroom, seafront apartment in the heart of the vibrant village of Strandhill. Private and self-contained, it's got a bedroom, bathroom, open-plan lounge, kitchen and dining area, plus everything you need on the doorstep.
Address: Seafront, Strandhill, Co. Sligo
Tel: +353 86 2625034
Web: www.airbnb.ie/rooms/20080230
Email: strandhillapartment@gmail.com

The Dunes Accommodation
Run by a local family, The Dunes offers en-suite rooms, free wifi and on-site parking. A central location in the picturesque village of Strandhill also means easy access to plenty of award winning restaurants, bars, live music venues and more.
Address: Top Road, Strandhill, Co. Sligo.
Tel: +353 87 9883644
Web: www.dunesaccommodation.com
Email: info@dunesaccommodation.com

FOOD AND DRINK

Eithna's By the Sea Seafood
Eithna's By the Sea Seafood shares delicious bounty from sea to shore. Here you will find the finest seafood, in award winning creations using only seasonal ingredients sourced direct from local suppliers on Sligo's Wild Atlantic Way.
Address: The Harbour, Mullaghmore, Co. Sligo
Tel: +353 71 9166407
Web: www.bythesea.ie
Email: info@bythesea.ie

Kate's Kitchen
Located in the heart of Sligo town, Kate's Kitchen is an independent grocery store and small café. With an in-house bakery, Kate's serves Fixx Coffee, homemade lunches packed with artisan foods, lifestyle gifts and cosmetics.
Address: 3 Castle Street, Co. Sligo
Web: www.kateskitchen.ie
Email: info@kateskitchen.ie

Pudding Row
A cosy café and bakery beside the sea in Easkey, Pudding Row serves an array of freshly baked artisan goods, all-day breakfasts and delicious lunches. Expect locally sourced and organic ingredients baked fresh each day, plus baking classes are available as well.
Address: Main St, Easkey, Co. Sligo
Tel: +353 96 49794
Web: www.puddingrow.ie
Email: hello@puddingrow.ie

Sweet Beat Café

Our riverside café serves up plant-based brunch, lunch and takeaways. Sweet Beat's menu is bursting with local and organic produce, from seasonal super salads and raw cakes to freshly baked goods paired with 3fe coffee, cold pressed juices and smoothies.

Address: Bridge Street, Co. Sligo
Tel: +353 71 9138795
Web: www.sweetbeat.ie
Email: hello@sweetbeat.ie

The Draft House

Quirky and engaging, this gastropub lives up to its slogan: "We don't do ordinary". Locals and visitors love the casual ingredients-led food, range of craft beers and laid-back vibe. A worthy winner of the Bord Bia 'Just Ask' award.

Address: Shore Road, Strandhill, Co. Sligo
Tel: +353 71 9122222
Web: www.thedrafthouse.ie
Email: info@thedrafthouse.ie

The Venue Bar & Restaurant

Located along the wild Atlantic Way, The Venue specialises in steak and local seafood. According to MyGuideIreland.com: "The food is marvellous, the view, spectacular: a dining experience not to be missed and not soon forgotten." Booking advised.

Address: Strandhill, Co. Sligo
Tel: +353 71 9168167
Web: www.venuestrandhill.ie
Email: ypvenue@gmail.com

ATTRACTIONS & ACTIVITIES

John G Coaching

Focusing on how to be, not just what to do. John offers a practical, non-fluffy approach to present-moment living, enabling clients to achieve confidence, calm and happiness. Coach, trainer and speaker, John works with businesses, schools, sports teams and individuals.

Address: Warriors Watch, Strandhill, Co. Sligo
Web: www.johngcoaching.com
Email: johngcoaching@gmail.com

Strandhill Surf School

Strandhill Surf School is a great place to learn to surf or improve your surfing skills. Located on the sea front, our highly qualified team of instructors run daily lessons for individuals and groups at this well-known surfing beach.

Address: Strandhill Surf School Beach Front, Strandhill, Sligo.
Tel: +353 71 9168483
Web: www.strandhillsurfschool.com
Email: strandhillsurfschool@gmail.com

Wild Wet Adventure

Kayaking, canoeing, stand up paddleboarding and guided walks. Located by the stunning shores of Lough Talt, Temple House Lakes and its surrounds, Wild Wet Adventures provides an introduction to water-based activities in a safe and enjoyable way.

Address: Lough Talt, Largan, Co. Sligo
Tel: +353 86 7222750
Web: www.wildwetadventures.ie
Email: john@wildwetadventures.ie

INDEX

USEFUL CONVERSION TABLES

OVEN TEMPERATURE CONVERSIONS

Farenheit	Centigrade	Gas Mark	Description
225 F	110 C	¼	Very Cool
250 F	130 C	½	
275 F	140 C	1	Cool
300 F	150 C	2	
325 F	170 C	3	Very Moderate
350 F	180 C	4	Moderate
375 F	190 C	5	
400 F	200 C	6	Moderately Hot
425 F	220 C	7	Hot
450 F	230 C	8	
475 F	240 C	9	Very Hot

US LIQUID MEASUREMENTS

1 gallon	4 quarts	3.79 L (can round to 4L)
1 quart	2 pints	.95 L (can round to 1L)
1 pint	2 cups	16 fl. oz. or 450 ml
1 cup	8 fl oz	225 ml (can round to 250ml)
1 tablespoon (Tbsp.)	½ fl oz	16 ml (can round to 15 ml)
1 teaspoon (tsp.)	⅓ tablespoon	5 ml

BRITISH LIQUID MEASUREMENTS

1 UK pint	0.56 ltrs	
1 UK liquid oz	0.96 US liquid oz	
1 pint	570 ml	16 fl oz
1 breakfast cup	10 fl oz	½ pint
1 tea cup	⅓ pint	
1 Tablespoon	15 ml	
1 dessert spoon	10 ml	
1 teaspoon	5 ml	⅓ Tablespoon
1 ounce	28.4 g	can round to 25 or 30
1 pound	454 g	
1 kg	2.2 pounds	

INTERNATIONAL LIQUID MEASUREMENTS

Country	Standard Cup	Standard Teaspoon	Standard Tablespoon
Canada	250 ml	5 ml	15 ml
Australia	250 ml	5 ml	20 ml
UK	250 ml	5 ml	15 ml
New Zealand	250 ml	5 ml	15 ml

thanks!

AS WITH ALL OF OUR PROJECTS, WE CAN'T PRODUCE THEM WITHOUT SOME HELP FROM OUR WONDERFUL FRIENDS AND COLLEAGUES.

Our biggest thanks goes out to the team at Shells. You have helped us grow and keep the Shells' buzz going while we've taken time out to enjoy Arlo, and to travel and glean inspiration for the new foods and flavours we've brought to Shells. Without our strong team none of these wonderful opportunities would have been possible, including the production of this book, which has been such a labour of love for us.

Secondly, our thanks goes out to the amazing community here. We have such a loyal following and your support is palpable. So many of our friends were ready to just drop and go as soon as we put a shout out about doing photos for the book: From jumping into the sea in the freezing cold (Lorna), to heading to the beach for a BBQ (Eddie) – the Strandhill crew never question, they just leap on board and join the madness.

We are also very lucky to work with all the crew at Orca Publications – especially the editor Louise and designer David, who bring our crazy ideas together into such a special book. And, thanks to Shannon for the words and Mike for the great photos, which makes it look so amazing.

Also thanks to Paula Mills, for supplying wonderful and original illustrations to help keep the vision and style of our books strong and creative.

And, of course, a big thanks to you, the reader. Without people buying our books we wouldn't be able to produce them. We hope you get as much inspiration, enjoyment and good food out of the book as we did making it.

Big Love

Jane, Myles & Arlo

Jane & Myles